Product Liability:
The new law under the
Consumer Protection Act 1987

Fourmat Publishing

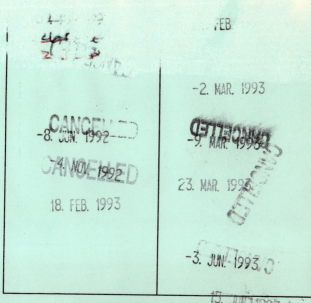

Product Liability:
The new law under the
Consumer Protection Act 1987

by
Rodney Nelson-Jones
and
Peter Stewart
partners in Field Fisher & Martineau, Solicitors

London
Fourmat Publishing
1987

ISBN 1 85190 034 9

First published July 1987

Reprinted January 1988

© 1987 R M Nelson-Jones and P J Stewart

Fourmat Publishing
27 & 28 St Albans Place Islington Green London N1 ONX

Printed in England by Billing & Sons Limited, Worcester

Preface

Product liability is liability for unfit, defective or dangerous products. "Product" normally denotes movable goods, such as chairs or cars, together with certain intangibles like gas and electricity. The liability of those associated with their manufacture or sale takes two main forms. The first, on which this book mostly concentrates, is liability to pay damages, enforceable through civil court action. The second is liability to criminal prosecution for breaches of statutes and safety regulations.

English law has long provided remedies for defective products. These may be claims for breach of contract and/or claims in tort (eg negligence). Increasingly, these have been perceived as inadequate in many circumstances, notably the thalidomide tragedy. Consequently there has been intense pressure from consumer bodies for the law to provide better protection. This has been combined with a desire on the part of the twelve Common Market countries to harmonise their laws on product liability.

After years of deliberation, the European Communities Council issued a Directive in July 1985. This was designed to provide greater protection for the consumer and to harmonise as far as possible the product liability laws of the member States. The Directive provided that each should introduce the necessary law to implement it by July 1988. The United Kingdom has done so through the Consumer Protection Act 1987 which received the Royal Assent on 15 May 1987 and will take effect after a transition period.

The purpose of this book is to consider product liability law in England and Wales on the basis of the Consumer Protection Act 1987 being in force. It is beyond its scope to deal directly with the relevant law in Scotland and Northern Ireland.

This book is primarily concerned with product liability in connection with consumer and other personal claims. Consequently product disputes between companies are not considered, except where an individual has a claim against two or more defendants which seek to allocate the liability amongst each other.

The authors aim to concentrate on the product liability provisions of the Consumer Protection Act 1987. Accordingly it is these that receive detailed attention. However, in order to appreciate the new law, it is necessary to understand the present law, which remains in force. This is outlined in Chapter 1. Then Chapters 2 to 5 consider the product liability provisions of the 1987 Act under the following heads: liability; defences; the effects of the new law, explained by means of case studies; and forum shopping and risk control. Finally, Chapter 6 deals with the consumer safety legislation under the present law and the 1987 Act.

Throughout the text, references to "the Act" are to the Consumer Protection Act 1987. Similarly, any reference to "Part I" is a reference to Part I of that Act.

The authors wish to express their gratitude to Ronald Walker QC for reading the first five chapters and advising; Trevor Hartley and Martin Buckley for their advice on international jurisdiction and company law respectively; David Ellis, Mark Lowe, Anne Morris, John Nelson-Jones, David Rawlins, David Smith and Janet Turner for reading parts of the text and commenting; Jill Wallace for her research and checking; and Jackie Charalambous and Danielle Prior for their typing. If, notwithstanding such distinguished support, any errors remain, the authors are of course responsible.

The law is stated as at 15 May 1987.

Rodney Nelson-Jones and Peter Stewart
Field Fisher & Martineau
Lincoln House
296-302 High Holborn
London WC1V 7JL

Contents

Table of Cases

Chapter 1

Introduction

Prior to the Consumer Protection Act 1987, product liability for consumer claims was based in two main areas of law: contract and tort. The Act supplements rather than replaces these laws. Since they remain in force, it is necessary to start with a short summary of them, in order to set the context within which the Act must be viewed. For the same purpose, the Directive is briefly introduced as the source of the Act. Consequently this chapter considers in turn:

- liability in contract;
- liability in tort;
- joint liability;
- time limits (limitation);
- the Directive.

1. Liability in contract

The law of contract applies to agreements for the performance of any obligation, including agreements to sell or hire goods. The type of contract with which this section is chiefly concerned is the agreement under which a consumer purchases or hires goods from someone in business. The safety and suitability of the product are often not explicitly considered, so the law implies terms into the contract in order to protect the consumer. The most significant statute in this context is the Sale of Goods Act 1979. Also relevant are the Supply of Goods (Implied Terms) Act 1973 and the Supply of Goods and Services Act 1982.

Section 2(1) of the Sales of Goods Act 1979 states that:

"A contract of sale of goods is a contract by which the seller transfers or agrees to transfer the property in goods to the buyer for a money consideration, called the price".

This covers the standard consumer purchases of food, household items, motor vehicles and the like. However, it does not apply to drugs supplied by pharmacists under the National Health Service: *Appleby* v *Sleep* (1968). Section 61(1) defines "goods" so as to include all tangible movable property except money, vegetable products resulting from agricultural labour, industrial growing crops and things severed from land (eg trees) under a contract of sale.

The most important implied terms are to be found in s.14 of the Sale of Goods Act 1979, which has replaced, with amendment, s.14 of the Sale of Goods Act 1893. Section 14(2) of the 1979 Act provides that:

"Where the seller sells goods in the course of a business, there is an implied condition that the goods supplied under the contract are of merchantable quality, except that there is no such condition -
(a) as regards defects specifically drawn to the buyer's attention before the contract is made; or
(b) if the buyer examines the goods before the contract is made, as regards defects which that examination ought to reveal".

Under s.14(2), the seller must be selling in the course of business. "Goods supplied" includes their containers: eg, *Morelli* v *Fitch and Gibbons* (1928), where a bottle of ginger wine broke at the neck when the plaintiff was opening it with a corkscrew.

The condition imposed is that of merchantable quality. An example of its breach is *Wren* v *Holt* (1903), in which beer bought by the plaintiff from the defendant's beer house contained arsenic and he was poisoned through drinking it. Section 14(6) defines merchantable quality:

"Goods of any kind are of merchantable quality within the

meaning of subsection (2) above if they are as fit for the purpose or purposes for which goods of that kind are commonly bought as it is reasonable to expect having regard to any description applied to them, the price (if relevant) and all the other relevant circumstances".

This imposes an objective test of reasonable fitness for common purpose(s). The condition applies to the sale of second hand as well as new goods, but with second hand goods a reasonable purchaser normally expects lower quality.

Although price is a relevant circumstance under s.14(6), the mere fact of cheapness does not justify the sale of unsafe goods. In *Godley* v *Perry* (1960), the six year old plaintiff purchased a catapult from the defendant's shop for 6d. While he was using it to fire a stone, the catapult broke and he was struck in his left eye. The catapult had been made with the cheapest kind of injection moulding material which proved unsuitable. It was held that the catapult was not of merchantable quality.

Section 14(3) lays down a further condition:

"Where the seller sells goods in the course of a business and the buyer, expressly or by implication, makes known -
(a) to the seller, or
(b) where the purchase price or part of it is payable by instalments and the goods were previously sold by a credit-broker to the seller, to that credit-broker,
any particular purpose for which the goods are being bought, there is an implied condition that the goods supplied under the contract are reasonably fit for that purpose, whether or not that is a purpose for which such goods are commonly supplied, except where the circumstances show that the buyer does not rely, or that it is unreasonable for him to rely, on the skill or judgement of the seller or credit-broker".

This is the condition of reasonable fitness for a particular purpose. "Particular" in this context means "specified or stated", rather than the opposite of "general": *Henry Kendall & Sons* v *Lillico & Sons Ltd* (1969). The buyer must reasonably rely on the skill or judgement of the seller. It is essential for the buyer to make the particular purpose known to the seller, if only by implication. In *Priest* v *Last* (1903), the plaintiff went to the defendant's shop, asked for a "hot water bottle" and inquired whether it would stand boiling water. The defendant told him that it was meant for hot water and he purchased it. Some days later the bottle burst in use, and the plaintiff's wife was scalded in consequence. It was held that the hot water bottle was not reasonably fit for the purpose for which it was sold.

This case may be contrasted with *Griffiths* v *Peter Conway Ltd* (1939). The plaintiff purchased from the defendant a Harris tweed coat which was specially made for her. She developed dermatitis soon after she began to wear it. This was due to the abnormal sensitivity of her skin. It was held that the particular purpose for which the coat was required was to be worn by a woman suffering from an abnormality and that, as this was not made known to the seller, he was not in breach of the condition.

Thus s.14 of the Sale of Goods Act 1979 implies two main conditions into sales by businesses. Under s.14(2), the goods must be of merchantable quality - reasonably fit for the purpose(s) for which such goods are commonly bought. Under s.14(3), they must be reasonably fit for any particular purpose made known to the seller. When this particular purpose is also a common purpose, s.14(2) and s.14(3) overlap. Reasonably fit does not mean absolutely fit. Despite this, the conditions in s.14 impose strict liability on the seller in that it is unnecessary for the buyer to prove fault on his part. In *Wren* v *Holt*, the publican was liable, although the arsenic in the beer could only have been discovered by chemical analysis. In *Ashington Piggeries Ltd* v *Christopher Hill Ltd* (1972), it was no defence that "in the then state of knowledge, scientific and commercial, no deliberate exercise of human skill or judgment could have prevented the meal from having its toxic effect on mink".

If either or both of the conditions in s.14(2) and 14(3) are broken, the buyer has two alternatives. Under s.11 he can repudiate the contract and reject the goods, provided that he has not already accepted them. Rejection of a product is most appropriate if it has not caused injury or damaged any other product, eg where a new washing machine simply breaks down. Section 35 states that:

> "The buyer is deemed to have accepted the goods when he intimates to the seller that he has accepted them, or (except where section 34 above otherwise provides) when the goods have been delivered to him and he does any act in relation to them which is inconsistent with the ownership of the seller, or when after the lapse of a reasonable time he retains the goods without intimating to the seller that he has rejected them".

If the buyer has accepted the goods, he is limited to claiming damages. This will in any event be his remedy of choice if he has been injured by them. Under s.53, the measure of damages is "the estimated loss directly and naturally resulting, in the ordinary course of events, from the breach".

Product liability does not arise only from the *sale* of goods. Goods supplied under other types of agreement are covered by the following statutes:

(a) Section 10 of the The Supply of Goods (Implied Terms) Act 1973 implies into hire purchase agreements the conditions of merchantable quality and reasonable fitness for any known particular purpose. If the retailer provides the credit, liability rests with him. If credit is provided by a finance company, it is this company which is liable.

(b) Section 4 of the Supply of Goods and Services Act 1982 implies the same terms into contracts for work and materials, where goods are supplied under, for instance, installation or repair contracts, such as the repair of a car or central heating system.

(c) Section 9 of the Supply of Goods and Services Act 1982 implies these terms into contracts for the hire of goods, eg rented televisions.

Retailers and others potentially liable for breach of the above conditions might desire to avoid liability through contract terms and notices. In sales to consumers, this is effectively prohibited by the Unfair Contract Terms Act 1977. Section 6(2) of this Act states that, as against a person dealing as a consumer, liability for breach of (*inter alia*) s.14 of the Sale of Goods Act 1979 and s.10 of the Supply of Goods (Implied Terms) Act 1973 cannot be excluded or restricted by reference to any contract term. Section 7(2) makes the same provision in relation to breaches of (*inter alia*) ss.4 and 9 of the Supply of Goods and Services Act 1982. Therefore businesses cannot avoid liability to consumers for breach of the conditions of merchantable quality and reasonable fitness for a known particular purpose. Between businesses, however, such terms are valid if reasonable.

A principal feature of liability in contract is that it is strict. It depends purely on breach of the contract, including its implied terms. It is unnecessary to prove fault on the part of the seller or anyone else. This is so even though the defect, as Lord Diplock expressed it in *Ashington Piggeries Ltd* v *Christopher Hill Ltd*, may have been "sheer bad luck". Moreover reliance on breach of contract is clearly appropriate where the product has not caused injury or damage, and redress is sought solely for the product having proved inadequate or defective.

The chief limitation of contractual liability results from the doctrine of privity of contract; in general, a contract cannot confer rights or impose obligations on any person except the parties to it. This has two aspects.

First, only someone who is a party to the contract can claim under it. In *Priest* v *Last*, the husband bought the hot water bottle and his wife was injured by it. He was entitled to recover expenses that he incurred in paying for her medical treatment but, as she was not a party to the contract, she could not claim damages for her injuries. If a purchaser buys a defective car which runs over an innocent pedestrian, the pedestrian cannot claim damages in contract.

Second, only someone who is privy to the contract can be sued under it. In sale of goods cases, this is the retailer. If the retailer is insolvent - and many small shops are not insured against or otherwise capable of meeting large claims - the purchaser has no further remedy in contract. Traditionally he has been left with an action in negligence, usually against the manufacturer.

Thus the law of contract is inherently limited in its scope. It covers the parties to the contract, but it neither protects nor imposes legal liabilities on anyone else.

2. Liability in tort

The confines of contract law mean that many of those injured by defective products have been forced to rely on the traditional laws of tort. A tort may be defined as a civil injury or wrong for which the appropriate remedy is an action for damages. In general, it is based on the concept of a defendant being at fault, although there are areas of strict liability where this is not required. In product liability cases there are four relevant areas of tort law, namely:

- the tort of negligence;
- breach of statutory duty;
- the tort of nuisance;
- the rule in *Rylands* v *Fletcher*.

Negligence

Much the most important of these is the tort of negligence. This connotes more than mere carelessness. It consists of a breach of a duty to take care owed to a person or persons who suffer damage in consequence. The damage must be reasonably foreseeable and not too remote.

The source of modern negligence law is the product liability case of *Donoghue* v *Stevenson* (1932). The plaintiff's friend purchased for her at a café a bottle of ginger beer. The bottle was made of dark opaque glass. She drank some of the ginger beer which has been poured into a tumbler. When the rest of the ginger beer was poured out, it was found to contain the remains of a decomposed snail. The plaintiff suffered shock and severe gastroenteritis. She could not sue the café owner, since she had no contract with him. Consequently she sued the manufacturer of the ginger beer.

The House of Lords held that she was entitled to recover damages from him. Lord Atkin enunciated the following fundamental product liability law principle:

> "...... a manufacturer of products, which he sells in such a form as to show that he intends them to reach the ultimate consumer in the form in which they left him with no reasonable possibility of intermediate examination, and with the knowledge that the absence of reasonable care in the preparation or putting up of the products will result in an injury to the consumer's life or property, owes a duty to the consumer to take that reasonable care."

Product

It soon became clear that the principle laid down by Lord Atkin in *Donoghue* v *Stevenson* was not limited to food and drink. The Privy Council rejected such a narrow interpretation in *Grant* v *Australian Knitting Mills Ltd* (1935), a case in which the appellant had contracted dermatitis due to excess sulphites in woollen underwear. Since then, the principle has been applied to an almost infinite range of products, such as vehicles, lifts, tombstones, hair dye, cleaning fluid, buildings and hazardous substances.

The principle covers defects resulting from extraneous substances, eg the snail in *Donoghue* v *Stevenson*. It applies to component parts and raw materials. It is also applicable to defective containers and packaging; in *Hill* v *James Crowe (Cases) Ltd* (1978), a lorry driver recovered damages when the wooden case on which he was standing broke. Thus there is no apparent limit to the types of product falling with the ambit of *Donoghue* v *Stevenson*.

Defendants

Manufacturers are the main category of defendant in product liability negligence cases. This contrasts with the law of contract, in which direct liability to the consumer rests with the retailer. Although *Donoghue* v *Stevenson* was a case against a manufacturer, its principle has since been extended to a wide variety of other defendants. Examples of further categories are listed below:

(a) Repairers, as in *Haseldine* v *Daw* (1941), where a firm of engineers was held liable for negligently repairing a lift which fell to the bottom of the shaft and injured the plaintiff visitor.

(b) Assemblers and erectors, eg a monumental mason who negligently erected a tombstone which fell on the plaintiff in a churchyard: *Brown* v *Cotterill* (1934).

(c) Installers, eg an electricity authority which wrongly connected wires when installing an electric meter in a factory, with the result that a fireman was electrocuted: *Hartley* v *Mayoh & Co* (1953).

(d) Importers and distributors, eg *Watson* v *Buckley Osborne Garrett & Co Ltd* (1940), a case of dermatitis due to hair dye produced by a Spanish company, in which the distributors were held liable for failing to test the product, and for advertising it as safe and harmless.

(e) Retailers, for instance where they create or aggravate a danger by negligent storage or when they fail to pass on a warning. In *Kubach* v *Hollands* (1937), chemists were held liable for supplying as manganese dioxide a substance which contained a mixture of antimony sulphide, with the result that a schoolgirl lost an eye in an experiment.

(f) Hirers, eg firms renting out cars or televisions, and also those who exchange goods: *Griffiths* v *Arch Engineering Co Ltd* (1968).

(g) Suppliers, eg a local authority which supplied water that became poisonous when passed through a lead pipe: *Barnes* v *Irwell Valley Water Board* (1939).

This list is not exhaustive. Other potential defendants include designers, testing agencies and, arguably, even endorsers of products.

Liability

The law of negligence does not impose a requirement of absolute safety. The duty on manufacturers and others concerned with products is to take reasonable care. In determining whether a defendant has exercised this, the courts will take into account the circumstances of the case, including in particular the following factors:

- the likelihood of an injury occurring;
- the extent of such injury, if an accident happens;
- whether the danger is concealed or obvious;
- any relevant safety standards;
- the benefits conferred by the product;
- the practicability and cost of eliminating the risk.

Thus the court must balance the various factors involved and decide what amounts to reasonable care in the particular circumstances. This standard must be assessed on the basis of what was known at the relevant time. As Lord Denning observed in *Roe* v *Minister of Health* (1954), "we must not look at the 1947 accident with 1954 spectacles". Accordingly "state of the art" evidence about standards and industrial practice at the time is admissible. This does not mean that ignorance of a risk is necessarily excusable, since a manufacturer is expected to conduct research into the safety of his products and to monitor reactions to them. In *Vacwell Engineering Co Ltd* v *BDH Chemicals Ltd* (1969), the manufacturers of a chemical called boron tribromide were held to be negligent for carrying out inadequate research, even though they had referred to four recent scientific books, when the chemical exploded in water and caused death.

The principle of vicarious liability means that a manufacturer or other defendant is liable for the negligence of his employees. He is not, however, vicariously liable for the negligence of sub-contractors such as component suppliers.

His duty here is to exercise reasonable care over their selection and to take proper steps to check the design and reliability of components. As Baker J confirmed in *Taylor* v *Rover Co Ltd* (1966), "He must take reasonable care by inspection or otherwise to see that those parts can properly be used to put his product in a condition in which it can be safely used or consumed in the contemplated manner by the ultimate user or consumer."

Defect

Product defects can conveniently be divided into three categories:

- design defects;
- manufacturing defects;
- marketing defects.

The distinctive feature of a *design* defect is that the defect exists although the product was manufactured as intended. Either the product should not have been manufactured at all, as with thalidomide; or it may lack sufficient safety devices, or its component materials are not strong enough or a combination of constituent factors leads to an adverse result. Such a defect is common to all the defendant's products of that type and may therefore result in multiple rather than isolated injuries. The significance of design defects was recognised by Lord Denning MR in *Williams* v *Trimm Rock Quarries Ltd* (1965), a case in which the manufacturers of a new type of drilling machine were held liable when the machine toppled over the edge of a quarry and killed the employee who was operating it. He said "Further, before sending a machine like this out for demonstration and putting it on the market, the toolmakers should have guarded against the possibility of its rising up and toppling over, and should have investigated those possible sources of danger."

Where a *manufacturing* defect occurs, in contrast, the product does not reach the consumer in its intended form. There is a better chance of the defect being confined to a single item, but it may affect a whole run. Typical problems include wrongly assembled machinery and unintended incorporation of foreign bodies or impurities, such as wire protruding from a sweet: *Barnett* v *H & J Packer & Co Ltd* (1940). Alternatively, the defect may be in a container or packaging. If a component is defective, primary liability usually rests with the component producer (if traceable), but, as seen above, the manufacturer of the finished product may also be deemed negligent in certain cases.

A *marketing* defect consists of a failure to provide adequate warnings or instructions. Warnings are needed when the product is dangerous but the danger is concealed, as with explosive or inflammable substances, or where the product is inherently hazardous to health, eg a jewellery cleaning fluid that caused injury on coming into contact with the plaintiff's eyes: *Fisher* v *Harrods Ltd* (1966). In cases of potential danger, directions for use should also warn of the consequences of failing to follow the directions. The need for accurate translation in the case of foreign goods is illustrated by *French* v *Olau Lines* (1983), in which a cleaner was injured by chlorine gas after mixing two cleaning agents contrary to warnings printed in foreign languages. The requirement of warnings may extend to cases when the defect only becomes apparent after sale. In extreme circumstances, only a recall will suffice: *Walton* v *British Leyland UK Ltd* (1978).

Evidence and causation

The burden of proving negligence and its necessary causal link with the injury is on the plaintiff, who must discharge it on the balance of probabilities. Accordingly a primary line of defence is that he has failed to do so. In seeking to overcome this, the plaintiff may rely on two evidential aids:

(a) the maxim *res ipsa loquitur* - the thing speaks for itself. Alternatively, the plaintiff may ask the court to draw obvious inferences from circumstantial evidence. In *Grant* v *Australian Knitting Mills Ltd*, it was held that "If excess sulphites were left in the garment, that could only be because someone was at fault. The appellant is not required to lay his finger on the exact person in all the chain who was responsible, or to specify what he did wrong".

(b) The principle stated by the House of Lords in *McGhee* v *National Coal Board* (1972). This is that where the defendant's fault materially increases the risk of a certain kind of injury, eg dermatitis, and injury of that kind subsequently occurs, the defendant is deemed to have caused it.

Nevertheless, proving causation can be a formidable barrier. This is particularly apparent in cases involving pharmaceutical products and vaccines in which arguments have often raged as to whether the claimant's injury was caused by the drug or vaccine, or whether it was due to constitutional causes and would have occurred in any event.

Defendants are entitled to adduce evidence that they have taken all reasonable care; if they have, they are not liable in negligence. They can allege that the product in question has not led to any other injury or complaint, and argue that their system is foolproof. To prove a safe system is not of itself sufficient, however, since a manufacturer can still be vicariously liable for the individual negligence of an employee.

Defences

In addition to the general points in the preceding section, the defendant may rely on more specific defences. One arising out of Lord Atkin's *dictum* in *Donoghue* v *Stevenson* is that he reasonably expected that there would be an intermediate examination capable of discovering the defect. In particular, a component producer is often entitled to expect this of the manufacturer of the finished product. Also it is sometimes reasonable for producers to expect intermediaries to pass on warnings. In *Holmes* v *Ashford* (1950) the manufacturers of a hair dye were held not liable on the grounds that they had warned the hairdresser of its potential danger, but he failed to test it and did not warn the plaintiff, who contracted dermatits.

Where damage has been caused by a component, the component producer or the finished product manufacturer may have the defence that the defect was the other's responsibility. In *Evans* v *Triplex Safety Glass Co Ltd* (1936), a car windscreen suddenly shattered and injured the occupants of the car. One of the grounds on which the producers of the windscreen were held not liable was that the glass may have been strained when screwed into its frame by the car manufacturers.

An important line of defence is that the defect was not present when the defendant supplied the product. For instance, it may be alleged that it only arose through lack of servicing or repair or through fair wear and tear. In *Evans* v *Triplex Safety Glass Co Ltd,* a further ground on which the plaintiff failed was that over a year had elapsed since the car was purchased, so that negligence could not necessarily be inferred.

Another defence is that the danger was so clear that there can be no cause for complaint. This is doubly effective if the danger is not only apparent but unavoidable. In *Crow* v *Barford* (1963) the plaintiff was using a motor mower with a large opening for grass ejection. He put his foot in the opening and was injured by the rotating blades. It was held that the manufacturers had not negligently designed the mower.

It is also a defence that injury or damage only occurred because the product was used in an unexpected or inappropriate manner. For instance, an aerosol container should not be banged on a concrete wall: *Rae and Rae* v *T Eaton & Co Ltd* (1961). And in *Heil* v *Hedges* (1951), a contract case, raw pork chops infected with a parasite were held not to be unfit on the ground that the plaintiff's maid had undercooked the meat and that, had she cooked it properly, the parasite would have been killed; accordingly the defendant butcher was not liable to the plaintiff for her resultant trichinosis.

Section 1 of the Law Reform (Contributory Negligence) Act

1945 provides that:

> "Where any person suffers damage as the result partly of his own fault and partly of the fault of any other person or persons, a claim in respect of that damage shall not be defeated by reason of the fault of the person suffering the damage, but the damages recoverable in respect thereof shall be reduced to such extent as the court thinks just and equitable having regard to the claimant's share in the responsibility for the damage."

Examples are failing to heed (even inadequate) warnings or instructions and continuing to use a product after learning that it is defective.

Limitation defences are considered separately; see page 30.

Damage

The main type of damage due to a defective product that gives rise to a claim in negligence is personal injury or death. Under the Congenital Disabilities (Civil Liabilities) Act 1976, pre-natal injury is also covered. The value of loss or damage to other property may be claimed. In addition, it has been accepted in a case involving collapse of a television mast that damage to the defective product itself can be recovered: *IBA* v *BICC Construction Ltd* (1980).

In general, it is not possible to recover damages for pure economic loss unaccompanied by any injury or property damage: *Muirhead* v *Industrial Tank Specialities Ltd* (1985). It is also thought that liability in tort does not arise if the sole complaint is that a product is shoddy or inadequate and it has not caused injury or damage. The remedy for this has been said to be in contract alone: Stamp LJ in *Dutton* v *Bognor Regis UDC* (1972).

Claimants

In *Donoghue* v *Stevenson*, Lord Atkin stated:

"You must take reasonable care to avoid acts or omissions which you can reasonably foresee would be likely to injure your neighbour. Who, then, in law is my neighbour? The answer seems to be - persons who are so closely and directly affected by my act that I ought reasonably to have them in contemplation as being so affected when I am directing my mind to the acts or omissions which are called in question."

Consequently the principle in *Donoghue* v *Stevenson* does not only apply to consumers of products. It has been extended to cover, for instance, employees, retailers, passengers and even bystanders. In *Stennett* v *Hancock and Peters* (1939), a pedestrian was allowed to recover damages from a motor repairer when a flange came off a moving lorry and struck her on the leg. Any person may claim for damage due to a defective product, provided that the defendant owed him a duty of care.

Other relevant torts

Breach of statutory duty is committed by breaking a duty imposed by an Act or Regulations. An action for damages will arise if the statute imposes a duty for the protection of a specific class of citizen. The damage must be of the kind that the statute was intended to prevent. Examples are:

(a) the Factories Act 1961, eg where the occupier fails to provide a safe lift as required by s.22;
(b) the Employers Liability (Defective Equipment) Act 1969 whereby an employee who suffers injury due to defective equipment supplied by his employer can recover damages from him, even if the employer had no reason to be aware of the defect;
(c) the Defective Premises Act 1972 requires, *inter alia*, any person carrying out work to a dwelling to see that the work is done with proper materials.

Although it does not give rise to a cause of action in tort, it is convenient to mention here the Vaccine Damage Payments Act 1979. This makes provision for a payment by the

Department of Health and Social Security to anyone who suffers severe disablement as a result of vaccination against certain specified diseases, such as whooping cough.

The tort of private nuisance occurs when a person is injured or otherwise prejudiced or disturbed in the enjoyment of land. The nuisance must have arisen elsewhere, so it usually results from acts done on neighbouring land. An example is where asbestos dust escapes from a factory and is breathed by neighbouring householders.

The rule formulated in the case of *Rylands* v *Fletcher* (1868) is that:

> "the person who for his own purposes brings on his lands and collects and keeps there anything likely to do mischief if it escapes, must keep it in at his peril, and if he does not do so is prima facie answerable for all the damage which is the natural consequence of its escape."

This rule overlaps with the tort of nuisance. It has been applied to the escape of gas, electricity, oil and poisonous waste.

3. Joint liability

The effect of joint and several liability, which is found under the existing laws of contract and tort, is that each defendant is liable for the full extent of the claim, even though there may be other defendants who are also liable. Consequently where Harvard Stores and Perfect Products are jointly and severally liable to Mr Green for his £10,000 claim, if he sues Harvard Stores alone they will have to pay the full £10,000.

Naturally, a defendant who satisfies a claim in full may wish to seek a contribution from other companies who are also liable. Rights to contribution may be contained in a contract between the companies. Apart from this, they are governed by the Civil Liability (Contribution) Act 1978. The most important provisions of the 1978 Act are as follows:

"Subject to the following provisions of this section, any person liable in respect of any damage suffered by another person may recover contribution from any other person liable in respect of the same damage (whether jointly with him or otherwise)." (s.1(1))
"Subject to subsection (3) below, in any proceedings for contribution under section 1 above the amount of the contribution recoverable from any person shall be such as may be found by the court to be just and equitable having regard to the extent of that person's responsibility for the damage in question." (s.2(1))

In the example above, s.1(1) entitles Harvard Stores to recover a contribution from Perfect Products. Section 2(1) provides that this will be whatever proportion of the £10,000 the judge thinks just and equitable having regard to their respective responsibility for the defective product. In some cases, the contribution can amount to 100%.

4. Time limits

These are set out in the Limitation Act 1980 which contains separate time limits for cases involving personal injury or death. Section 11 provides that, where a claimant suffers personal injury, he must commence court action within 3 years of:

- the date on which the cause of action accrued; or
- the date of his knowledge (if later).

Section 14 states that the date of knowledge is the date on which he first knew or might reasonably have been expected to ascertain that:

(a) his injury was significant; and
(b) the injury was attributable to the relevant act or omission; and
(c) the identity of the defendant; and
(d) if it is alleged that the act or omission was that of a person other than the defendant, the identity of that person and the additional facts supporting the bringing

of an action against the defendant.

Sections 12 and 13 apply the above rules to fatal cases. The operation of the rules is illustrated by *Simpson* v *Norwest Holst (Southern) Ltd* (1980). The plaintiff was injured at work on 4 August 1976 and wished to sue his employers. His contract of employment described them as the "Norwest Holst Group". On 4 July 1979 his solicitors were told that they were in fact Norwest Holst (Southern) Ltd. Court proceedings were started on 17 August 1979, about three years and a fortnight after the accident. It was held that, as the plaintiff could not reasonably have been expected to know his employers' identity by 17 August 1976, his court action was not time barred.

Section 33 gives the court a discretion to disapply the three year time limit where it considers that it would be equitable to do so. It must take into account all the circumstances of the case and in particular such factors as the length of and reasons for the plaintiff's delay and the extent to which the delay has reduced the cogency of the evidence. In *Buck* v *English Electric Co Ltd* (1977), the plaintiff knew by 1959 that he had pneumoconiosis. He was able to remain in full time work and felt that he would be "sponging" if he sued his employers. He only did so in 1975 after his condition deteriorated. His widow was allowed to proceed with the court action because the judge found his reasons for delay sympathetic and, since his employers had been confronted by several similar claims in the meantime, it was held that the cogency of evidence in this case had not been reduced by the delay.

In cases not involving personal injuries - eg where the sole claim is for loss of or damage to property - the traditional time limit for an action founded on tort was confirmed by s.2 of the Limitation Act 1980 as six years from the date on which the cause of action accrued (ie when damage occurred). This created problems when the damage did not become manifest until later. Consequently, the Latent Damage Act 1986 created new time limits for negligence actions in cases of latent damage not involving personal injuries. It has achieved this by inserting sections into the 1980 Act.

Section 14A of the Limitation Act 1980 provides that in negligence actions for latent damage not involving personal injuries, the limitation period is either:

(a) six years from the date on which the cause of action accrued; or

(b) three years from the date on which the plaintiff or any person in whom the cause of action was vested before him first had the knowledge required for bringing an action in damages and a right to bring it, if that period expires later than the period in (a).

Section 14B provides in such cases a longstop limitation period of fifteen years from the date of the negligent act or omission that has caused the damage. This overrides the time limits in s.14A, even if the damage has not occurred or is not manifest by the end of the fifteen years.

A single example may illustrate the effect of ss.14A and 14B. Suppose that the negligent act is committed in 1987 and that damage results from it in 1988. If the damage is immediately patent, the limitation period expires in 1994. If the damage is discoverable in 1993, time runs out in 1996. If the damage only becomes discoverable in 2001, s.14B operates to bar court action after 2002.

When the claim is founded on simple contract for property loss or damage only, s.5 provides a limitation period of six years from the date on which the cause of action accrued, ie the date of breach of contract. Section 10 states that the time limit for contribution proceedings under the Civil Liability (Contribution) Act 1978 is two years from the date of judgment or settlement. Section 28 provides for the limitation periods to be extended where the plaintiff is under 18 or a patient incapable of administering his affairs. Section 32 provides for their postponement in cases of fraud, concealment or mistake.

It follows from the above that, if a defective product causes injury, manufacturers and other potential defendants are at risk of being sued many years after it is made, supplied or purchased. Indeed, the effect of s.33 is that there is no absolute maximum limit in personal injury cases. If the product only causes property loss or damage, s.14B provides an overriding maximum limit of fifteen years in negligence cases. If a property damage claim is founded in contract, retailers possess the modest protection of the six year limitation period imposed by s.5.

5. The Directive

Public concern at the problems experienced by the thalidomide claimants in trying to recover damages under the existing laws of contract and tort led to renewed pressure for their reform. Simultaneously the Common Market was seeking to harmonise the product liability laws of member States. It was deemed an important area for harmony, since differing legal liability in member States affects the price to be charged for a product and distorts competition.

The Commission to the Council of Ministers of the European Communities embarked upon the task in 1972. It submitted a draft Directive in 1976 and a revised draft in 1979. On 25 July 1985 an agreed text of the Directive was adopted, with the requirement that member States implement it in their national laws within 3 years, ie by July 1988.

The main aims of the Directive are twofold: to harmonise product liability law within the European Communities, and to increase consumer protection. These aims are illustrated by the following passages from the introduction to the Directive:

> "Whereas approximation of the laws of the Member States concerning the liability of the producer for damage caused by the defectiveness of his products is necessary because the existing divergences may distort competition and affect the movement of goods within the common market and entail a differing degree of protection of the consumer

against damage caused by a defective product to his health or property;

Whereas liability without fault on the part of the producer is the sole means of adequately solving the problem, peculiar to our age of increasing technicality, of a fair apportionment of the risks inherent in modern technological production;".

Part I of the Act implements the Directive. The Act has five Parts in all:

- Part I sets out the circumstances in which, under its operation, a consumer can make a claim for damage caused by a defective product.
- Part II contains the consumer safety legislation.
- Part III deals with misleading price indications, which are outside the scope of this book.
- Part IV details the methods of enforcing the legislation in Parts II and III.
- Part V consists of miscellaneous provisions concerning, for example, the definition of certain terms.

In addition, there are five Schedules of which the first, the most important, sets out the time limits for starting court action under the Act.

Chapter 2

Liability under the new Act

Lord Denning has compared the impact of European Communities law on the UK to an incoming tide flowing into our estuaries and up our rivers (*Bulmer* v *Bollinger* (1974)). Into the river of UK product liability law has flowed the EC Directive of 25 July 1985. Within its three year time limit, it has been implemented by the Consumer Protection Act 1987. Part I is devoted to product liability.

Section 1(1) of the Act states "This Part shall have effect for the purpose of making such provision as is necessary in order to comply with the product liability Directive and shall be construed accordingly". This not only confirms the European provenance of the new law. It also means that, if UK courts encounter difficulties in interpreting the new Act, they may refer to the Directive for elucidation. The words "shall be construed accordingly" are mandatory. In cases of doubt, the Act must be interpreted so as to comply with the Directive.

Article 1 of the Directive states the essence of the new law with classic brevity: "The producer shall be liable for damage caused by a defect in his product". This is the principle of strict liability. The Act implements it by, in effect, defining and giving substance to each of its main words: product, producer, liable, defect, damage. This chapter follows a similar pattern.

1. Meaning of "product"

The preamble to the Directive provides "Whereas liability

without fault should apply only to movables which have been industrially produced ......". Thus two criteria must be met for an article to constitute a product. It must be movable; and it must have been industrially produced. Cars and ovens are products. Buildings are not.

Section 1(2) defines "product" as follows:

> ""product" means any goods or electricity and ...... includes a product which is comprised in another product, whether by virtue of being a component part or raw material or otherwise."

By s.45:

> ""goods" includes substances, growing crops and things comprised in land by virtue of being attached to it and any ship, aircraft or vehicle."

Section 45 also states:

> ""substance" means any natural or artificial substance, whether in solid, liquid or gaseous form or in the form of a vapour, and includes substances that are comprised in or mixed with other goods".

Thus "product" obviously includes standard consumer goods such as lawnmowers and televisions. It also includes components, such as brakes in a car. It includes raw materials incorporated into goods. It includes ships, hovercrafts, aeroplanes, gliders, trains and other vehicles. It includes gas, water and electricity. It includes waste when supplied as a product in its own right, but not where it is merely an unwanted incident of the production process, eg effluent from a factory.

Land and buildings are not products, because they are immovable. However, s.45 clearly covers such items as bricks, wood and cement, even though they become part of a house. Thus building materials are products, but not the building itself; the effect is that the Act applies to building material producers but not normally to the work of building and civil engineering contractors. If your house falls down due to defective bricks, you may sue under Part I of the Act. If it falls down due to defective design or assembly, you must rely on the existing laws of contract and tort (including the Defective Premises Act 1972).

Nuclear accidents are excluded from the scope of the Act. Article 14 of the Directive states: "This Directive shall not apply to injury or damage arising from nuclear accidents and covered by international conventions ratified by the Member States". In the UK the relevant conventions are mainly implemented by the Nuclear Installations Act 1965. Accordingly s.6(8) of the Act provides "Nothing in this Part shall prejudice the operation of section 12 of the Nuclear Installations Act 1965 (rights to compensation for certain breaches of duties confined to rights under that Act)".

The more contentious exception concerns agricultural produce. Section 1(2) defines this as meaning "any produce of the soil, of stockfarming or of fisheries". Thus it evidently includes fruit, fish, vegetables, meat and wine. An area of uncertainty is vegetables grown by hydroponic culture, in which soil is not involved, such as certain cucumbers, tomatoes and lettuces. The UK government intends the produce of hydroponic culture to be deemed agricultural produce, but the matter is not free from doubt.

Section 2(4) states that the strict liability provisions of Part I shall not "apply to a person in respect of any defect in any game or agricultural produce if the only supply of the game or produce by that person to another was at a time when it had not undergone an industrial process".

Lord Lucas of Chilworth has stated on behalf of the government that for liability under Part I to attach in respect of game or agricultural produce:

> "The test is twofold. First, there must have been processing, and for processing to take place some essential characteristic of the product must have been

37

altered. Simply cutting sprouts from a sprout plant or harvesting potatoes does not constitute a process. Those processes do not change the essential characteristics of the product. Moreover, the process must be an industrial one - that is, it must be carried on on a large and continuing scale and with the intervention of machinery. I have in mind the processes that turn peas into frozen peas or potatoes into frozen chips. But what is important is that we should not completely destroy the value of the exemption for primary agricultural produce by making suspect all those processes which necessarily and traditionally have been carried out on farms - harvesting, washing and sometimes packaging - and which do not interfere with the inherent nature of the product."

When asked in the House of Commons about injections of hormones and tenderising substances into animals, Mr Michael Howard, the Parliamentary Under-Secretary of State for Trade and Industry, answered:

"industrial processing ...... does not apply to things done to the animal while it is alive, which includes veterinary medicines, and so on. It is designed to remove from the exemption things done later to the primary agricultural product such as canning or other methods of preservation."

In summary, primary agricultural produce is outside Part I, but industrially processed agricultural produce is within it. A fisherman is not liable for selling sickly fish, but a food manufacturer would be liable for producing defective fish fingers. If contaminated wheat eventually forms part of defective biscuits, it is the biscuit manufacturer rather than the wheat grower who will be liable under Part I. The industrial manufacturers then have to exercise their rights of contribution and indemnity against the producers of the primary foodstuffs. If a consumer is directly injured by primary agricultural produce, such as rotten tomatoes, Part I does not apply at all and he must rely on the existing law. The European Communities member States have a right to derogate from this provision, although none has yet done so, and its continuation is to be reviewed by the EC Commission in 1995.

2. Defendants

The nucleus of Part I of the Act is s.2(1):

> "Subject to the following provisions of this Part, where any damage is caused wholly or partly by a defect in a product, every person to whom subsection (2) below applies shall be liable for the damage."

This not only states the principle of strict liability. It also indicates the range of possible defendants. These are considered in the following order:

- s.1(2) defines three types of producer;
- s.2(2) creates three categories of defendant - producers as defined in s.1(2), own-branders and EC importers;
- s.2(3) adds another category of defendant - suppliers, in certain defined circumstances.

Producers

Liability under Part I mainly rests with producers. Section 1(2) states:

> ""producer", in relation to a product means -
> (a) the person who manufactured it;
> (b) in the case of a substance which has not been manufactured but has been won or abstracted, the person who won or abstracted it;
> (c) in the case of a product which has not been manufactured, won or abstracted but essential characteristics of which are attributable to an industrial or other process having been carried out (for example, in relation to agricultural produce), the person who carried out that process."

The first and main type of producer is a manufacturer. As products include components and raw materials, producers include manufacturers not only of finished products but also of the components and raw materials comprised in them, eg not only car manufacturers but also manufacturers of brakes and windscreens.

The second type is involved with products which are not manufactured but which are mined or otherwise obtained. Examples are the mining of coal or gold or the obtaining of natural gas or North Sea oil.

The third type of producer is a processor. To qualify, a processor must have altered the essential characteristics of the product. Thus a processor does not become a producer merely by virtue of packaging goods. However it is thought that, for instance, pea canners will be classed as producers. So will those who refine petroleum or who process iron ore before it is put into a blast furnace. An agricultural example is processing a chicken into a self-basting bird.

Section 2(2) defendants

Section 2(2) defines the defendants to which s.2(1) refers as:

"(a) the producer of the product;
(b) any person who, by putting his name on the product or using a trade mark or other distinguishing mark in relation to the product, has held himself out to be the producer of the product;
(c) any person who has imported the product into a member State from a place outside the member States in order, in the course of any business of his, to supply it to another."

The first category has been considered above. It covers the manufacturers of finished products, components and raw materials, those who have won or abstracted substances, and processors of other products who have altered their essential characteristics.

The second category comprises "own-branders"; those who, even though they did not manufacture the defective product, represent themselves as its producer by putting their distinguishing feature on it. The EC Commission stated that this provision is intended to cover primarily those undertakings, such as mail order firms, which have products made by unspecified undertakings in accordance with precise instructions and sell them under their own name. To qualify, a person must (i) put his name or distinguishing mark on a product and (ii) hold himself out as its producer. Thus a department store would be *prima facie* liable for its branded goods, but it would be otherwise if the brander identifies the manufacturer on the label. Concern was expressed in the House of Lords about a pharmacist putting his name on a bottle of pills produced by one of the major drug companies; as long as he does nothing to hold himself out as the producer, he will not be an own-brander.

The third category covers importers into the EC from outside it. This provision is intended to safeguard consumers by ensuring that they are not forced to sue producers in distant foreign lands which may have poor legal systems. It applies to those who import into the EC, not to those who import into the UK from the EC. Thus if a compact disc player is imported from Singapore into France and is finally sold in the UK, liability under Part I will attach to the French importer from Singapore rather than the UK importer from France. The provision is limited to business supply. It does not cover a returning tourist selling to a friend; nor does it apply to industrial equipment imported for use rather than resale.

Article 3(2) of the Directive states: "Without prejudice to the liability of the producer, any person who imports into the Community a product ...... shall be responsible as a producer." Thus an EC importer is liable in addition to, not instead of, a foreign producer. This is confirmed by the Department of Trade and Industry in their explanatory note on the Directive:

"Those liable include the manufacturer of a finished product or component; the producer of raw material; or a person who holds himself out to be a producer (eg by

LIABILITY UNDER THE NEW ACT

putting an own-brand label on the article). Where an article is manufactured outside the EC, the importer will also be liable."

Therefore Part I applies in principle to, for instance, a Japanese or Canadian producer as well as to a French or English importer. Whether in practice the UK courts will assume jurisdiction over a non-EC company is considered in Chapter 5.

Section 2(3) defendants

Section 2(3) extends the range of possible defendants even further:

"Subject as aforesaid, where any damage is caused wholly or partly by a defect in a product, any person who supplied the product (whether to the person who suffered the damage, to the producer of any product in which the product in question is comprised or to any other person) shall be liable for the damage if -
(a) the person who suffered the damage requests the supplier to identify one or more of the persons (whether still in existence or not) to whom subsection (2) above applies in relation to the product;
(b) that request is made within a reasonable period after the damage occurs and at a time when it is not reasonably practicable for the person making the request to identify all those persons; and
(c) the supplier fails, within a reasonable period after receiving the request, either to comply with the request or to identify the person who supplied the product to him."

This subsection is of major importance to retailers and other intermediaries. Any person who supplied the product (whether to the victim, or to the producer of the final product, or to anyone else along the chain of supply) will himself be liable if three conditions are fulfilled:

(a) the victim requests the supplier to identify one or more of the producer, own-brander or EC importer (whether or not the firm in question has gone into liquidation or been dissolved);

(b) the request is made within a reasonable period after the damage occurs - the Act obviously contemplates that it may be an unreasonable or even impossible period after the product was produced - and at a time when the victim cannot reasonably be expected to identify all (not just some) of the other defendants;

(c) the supplier fails within a reasonable period to comply with the victim's request or to identify his own supplier. Thus the supplier has a fallback response; if he cannot identify the requested producer, own-brander or EC importer, it suffices for him to identify his own supplier. What is a reasonable period, and what exactly amounts to identification, will be for the courts to decide on the facts of each case.

Section 2(3) constitutes the Act's answer to what has been termed the problem of the unknown defendant. It protects the victim from anonymous or counterfeit products. He is permitted to proceed backwards along the chain of supply until he finally arrives at the producer, own-brander or EC importer. If this proves impossible, he is entitled to sue, subject to the reasonable period criteria, the supplier who has failed to comply with his request for their identification.

Section 1(3) limits this duty to identifying the producer etc of the finished product, not of its components. It states:

"For the purposes of this Part a person who supplies any product in which products are comprised, whether by virtue of being component parts or raw materials or otherwise, shall not be treated by reason only of his supply of that product as supplying any of the products so comprised."

A retailer who sells a car with a defective windscreen is only required to identify the producer or importer of the car, not the producer of the windscreen.

The operation of these subsections is illustrated by the following example. CP produces a defective valve in Taiwan. Pr incorporates this into a television in Singapore. Im imports it into the EC. He supplies it to Wh who supplies it to Re who sells it to Mr V. The television explodes and injures Mrs V. Meanwhile Pr goes out of business. Mrs V requests R to identify CP, Pr and Im. He does not have to identify CP and fails to identify Pr or Im, but tells Mrs V that his supplier was Wh. She promptly makes the same requests of Wh, who has destroyed all his records and cannot comply with it. As he fails to identify Pr or Im (his supplier), Wh is liable to Mrs V under Part I.

"Supply" is an important concept in the Act. Liability under s.2(3) depends on it. Moreover, the fact and date of supply are frequently relevant to the specified defences and time limits. Section 46 defines supplying goods as:

"doing any of the following, whether as principal or agent, that is to say -
(a) selling, hiring out or lending the goods;
(b) entering into a hire-purchase agreement to furnish the goods;
(c) the performance of any contract for work and materials to furnish the goods;
(d) providing the goods in exchange for any consideration (including trading stamps) other than money;
(e) providing the goods in or in connection with the performance of any statutory function; or
(f) giving the goods as a prize or otherwise making a gift of the goods;"

Thus, in the above example, the same result would have occurred if the television had been rented out to Mr V or won by him in a competition.

Section 6(2) extends s.2(3) to fatal cases. If the victim dies his personal representative (ie executor or administrator) can make the request. If the death is due to the defect, the request may also be made by any of the victim's dependants or relatives (as defined in the Fatal Accidents Act 1976).

Consequently, if the explosion had killed Mrs V, the request could have been made by Mr V, her personal representative (if different), or relatives such as her parents or sisters.

As the Department of Trade and Industry pointed out in their explanatory note:

"The position of pharmacists, doctors, nurses and others operating in the health sector requires particular consideration. Many doctors and health care personnel are the last link in the chain of supply of medicines from manufacturer to patient, and as such might be liable ...... when the producer of a defective medicinal product could not be identified. However, for NHS staff, the supplier would be the health authority, not the member of staff concerned. It is expected that the authority's records would need to provide particulars of the sources of its drugs if it is to be sure of avoiding liability ...... Some health care personnel such as general medical and dental practitioners are not employees of the health authorities but are self-employed and under contract to the authorities. Their position is similar to that of retail pharmacists who would be expected to maintain adequate records or, in the absence of such records, to be subject to liability when the producer cannot be identified."

Section 9 applies Part I of the Act to the Crown. This covers, in particular, government departments and thus includes certain medicines supplied under the National Health Service. The Crown may either be sued as a producer under s.2(2) or as a supplier under s.2(3). The limits of the Crown's liability are set out in the Crown Proceedings Act 1947.

3. Liability

The principle of strict liability is contained in s.2(1):

"Subject to the following provisions of this Part, where any damage is caused wholly or partly by a defect in a product, every person to whom subsection (2) below applies shall be liable for the damage."

The person who suffered the damage does not have to prove negligence. Nor need he have entered into a contract with the producer or supplier. Indeed any injured person may sue. It is irrelevant whether he was using the product. He may have been a mere bystander.

Thus the producer is liable to anyone who suffers damage due to a defect in his product. He is liable in full to the victim even when the damage is only partly due to the defect. His liability is not reduced when the damage is caused both by the defect and by the fault of a third party, eg if his defective pork pie is kept in unhygienic conditions by the retailer, thereby making it even worse.

It has been seen above that liability under s.2(2) may attach to a range of defendants: the producer of the finished product, the producer of the defective component part or raw material, an own-brander, the EC importer. In some cases, two or more may be liable. Section 2(5) deals with this by providing that "Where two or more persons are liable by virtue of this Part for the same damage, their liability shall be joint and several". This means that each is liable to the victim for the full extent of his damage, although he cannot recover this more than once. If a car with defective brakes causes damage, the producer of the car and the producer of the brakes are liable under Part I. The injured person may recover full damages from either or both. Thus he has complete choice as to whom to sue.

Section 2(6) states that "This section shall be without prejudice to any liability arising otherwise than by virtue of this Part". Accordingly the existing laws of contract and tort remain in force. A contracting consumer retains his rights against his supplier, notably under the Sale of Goods Act 1979, and any injured person may also sue anyone who is liable in negligence or other tort. Suppose that a defective refrigerator is manufactured in Hong Kong, imported into the EC by a Belgian firm, sold by it to English distributors who ought to have discovered the defect by inspection and testing, and supplied by them to London retailers who sold it to the victim. The victim may then sue any one or more of: the Hong Kong producer and the Belgian importer under the Act; the English distributors in the tort of negligence; and the London retailers for breach of contract (s.14 of the Sale of Goods Act 1979).

Justice between defendants is to be achieved through the Civil Liability (Contribution) Act 1978. Section l(l) provides that any person liable in respect of any damage may recover a contribution from any other person liable in respect of the same damage (whether jointly or otherwise). Section 2(1) states that the amount of the contribution recoverable from any person shall be whatever is just and equitable having regard to the extent of his responsibility for the damage. In the above example, it might be held that responsibility rests with the Hong Kong producer of the refrigerator and the English distributor who should have discovered the defect. If sued by the victim, the Belgian importer or the London retailer ought to be able to recover a full contribution from them. Equally, if only one of the Hong Kong producer and the English distributor is sued, he may be able to recover a proportionate contribution from the other. This is subject to whatever valid contract terms there may be allocating the liability between them.

Two distinctions are worth drawing. First, while the victim does not have to prove fault under Part I of the Act, fault in so far as it forms part of responsibility, continues to be relevant in the allocation of the victim's damages amongst defendants. Second, while liability under Part I to the victim cannot be limited or excluded by any contract term, businesses may continue to enter into contracts which limit and exclude their liability to each other. For example, whilst the producer of a defective product cannot avoid his liability to pay damages to the injured person, he can still recover an indemnity from his distributor (however innocent) if that is what their contract states.

4. Meaning of "defect"

Section 3(1) defines a defect:

> "Subject to the following provisions of this section, there is a defect in a product for the purposes of this Part if the safety of the product is not such as persons generally are entitled to expect; and for those purposes "safety", in relation to a product, shall include safety with respect to products comprised in that product and safety in the context of risks of damage to property, as well as in the context of risks of death or personal injury".

Thus the definition of defect is based on the expected safety of the product. It is irrelevant whether the product is unfit or unsuitable for its intended purpose, concepts that continue to apply in contract law. The level of safety is to some extent objective; it depends on what persons "generally are entitled to expect", not what the particular consumer did expect, and it is not intended to fluctuate according to individual allergies and susceptibilities. Compliance with safety standards is relevant but not conclusive; if a standard is out of date or sets only minimal requirements, a higher level of safety may be expected. Safety in relation to a product includes safety with respect to its components: the tubes and transistors, as well as the television. Moreover safety includes not only personal safety but also safety for property; persons generally are entitled to expect not only that a product will not injure them but also that it will not damage their property.

The Department of Trade and Industry explanatory note points out that:

> "The safety which a person is entitled to expect raises particularly complex issues in respect of medicinal products and adverse reactions to them. Establishing the existence of a defect in a medicine administered to a patient is complicated by the fact that not only is the human body a highly complex biological organism, but at the time of treatment it is already subject to an adverse pathological condition. In order to avoid an adverse

reaction, a medicine will have to be able to cope successfully with already faulty organs, disease, and almost infinite variations in individual susceptibility to the effect of medicines from person to person. The more active the medicine, and the greater its beneficial potential, the more extensive its effects are likely to be, and therefore the greater the chances of an adverse effect. A medicine used to treat a life threatening condition is likely to be much more powerful than a medicine used in the treatment of a less serious condition, and the safety that one is reasonably entitled to expect of such a medicine may therefore be correspondingly lower".

Section 3(2) states:

"In determining for the purposes of subsection (1) above what persons generally are entitled to expect in relation to a product all the circumstances shall be taken into account, including -
(a) the manner in which, and purposes for which, the product has been marketed, its get-up, the use of any mark in relation to the product and any instructions for, or warnings with respect to, doing or refraining from doing anything with or in relation to the product;
(b) what might reasonably be expected to be done with or in relation to the product; and
(c) the time when the product was supplied by its producer to another;
and nothing in this section shall require a defect to be inferred from the fact alone that the safety of a product which is supplied after that time is greater than the safety of the product in question".

The first set of circumstances concerns the presentation of the product. The manner and purpose of its marketing refers not only to its supply but also to its promotion, advertising and training in use. Its get-up covers styling, packaging and leaflets. Marks include trade marks. Instructions and warnings must cover both what to do and what not to do; it is necessary not only to instruct consumers how to use a 12 volt electric razor but also to tell them not to plug it into the mains. Inadequate instructions can make a product unsafe so importers from outside the EC, who are themselves liable as if they are producers, will need to check that any literature supplied with a product is accurately translated. If Japanese instructions on how to put a car into neutral are mistranslated so that if the driver follows the translation he puts the car into reverse, the EC importer will be liable under the Act for any resultant damage. The importance attached to product presentation in determining a defect means that exaggeration of a product's harmlessness is undesirable. It is preferable to indicate its potential hazards. If a bottled gas container is marked "highly flammable", it will not be considered defective if it burns due to being warmed up over a kitchen stove.

The second set of circumstances involves the reasonably expected use of the product. It is not specified whose the reasonable expectation is to be: the producer's, the purchaser's, or persons generally. Perhaps the answer is that it is to be the expectation of any reasonable person applying his mind to the matter. The second set is not to be considered in isolation from the first, since the presentation of a product and in particular its instructions do much to determine its reasonably expected use. A classic example is that of the American lady who attempted to dry her poodle in a microwave oven with the result that the poodle disintegrated after 90 seconds. It is submitted that, under Part I, UK courts would not deem the oven to be defective since its use was so entirely unexpected. More marginal cases are identified by the Department of Trade & Industry note:

"Raw materials, such as wood, would not normally be regarded as defective in the sense that they can be used quite safely for many different purposes. However, if it should be established that their use for a particular purpose was dangerous, then the question of whether the raw material supplier is liable will depend largely on the presentation and manner of marketing of the primary material, including any indications of use, warnings etc".

The third special circumstance is the time when the product was supplied by its producer to another. It is the time of supply, rather than the time of manufacture, that is most important. After manufacture, but before delivery, a producer may learn of further safety features which could be incorporated into his product; if he disregards them, he runs an increased risk of the product being deemed defective. It is the time of supply by the producer, not by the retailer, that is material; if a producer learns of the further safety features after he delivers his product to a wholesaler or retailer, this does not automatically result in his product being defective, even if he acquired his extra knowledge before the retailer sells the product to a customer. It follows from the emphasis on the time of the producer's supply that extra knowledge by the date of the accident is irrelevant for this purpose. The Law Commission has stated "Nor do we think it would be fair to apply the safety standards of 1977 to products put into circulation in 1967. For example, it would not be right to regard a 1967 car as defective merely on the ground that it was not produced with safety belts attached". If a product is manufactured in 1987, supplied by the producer to his distributor in 1988, sold to the customer in 1989 and causes damage in 1990, it is the entitled expectation of safety in 1988 to which s.3(2)(c) refers. A feature of this approach is that a defective product, if sufficiently safe at the time of its producer's supply, may continue to be offered for sale by retailers to customers without attracting liability under Part I.

Although three categories of circumstance are specifically mentioned, all the circumstances are to be taken into account in determining a defect. Thus miscellaneous factors may also be considered, including, where applicable, the concept of fair wear and tear.

Special problems arise over products concerned with information, such as books, tapes and letters. An example is an architect who gives advice in a letter about an alteration to a house. The letter is a product, because the notepaper on which it is written is a movable good, and if the paper proves poisonous to the touch there is no doubt that the letter is defective. Suppose, however, that the architect's advice is negligent and that in consequence the houseowner makes a faulty alteration that subsequently causes injury. The legislature intends that the architect's advice should not be regarded as a product merely because it appears on one and that the letter should not be deemed a defective product merely because bad advice has been typed onto it. Provided that this is correct, it follows that printers and bookbinders, for instance, are not to be held liable under the Act for reproducing errors in the material provided to them. Liability in the above example attaches to the architect under the tort of negligence.

Negligent advice is one problem. Printing errors are another. Mr Clement Freud MP gave the following example in the House of Commons:

"I have in my constituency ...... a prestigious printer ..... which is concerned that it may be blamed for textual errors in its printing. The British Printing Industries Federation wrote to the Minister and received a reply which said: 'It seems to us reasonably clear that the Directive does not apply to mis-statement'. I would simply like the Minister to make it clear that it is not the intention of the Bill to do so ...... In 1979 L published a chemical textbook in which it got wrong a proportion between two totally unpronounceable chemical elements; it printed that the proportion should be 2:30 instead of 2:3. A school had a major explosion as a result. Of course L, who printed the book, would be responsible. I would simply like the Minister to say that it is not an intention of the legislation to hold a printer responsible for textual errors".

Mr M Howard, the Minister in question, gave the required assurance that the Act is not intended to refer to such printing errors. Any remedy against the printers is to be sought under the law of negligence.

5. Damage

Section 5 defines the damage that gives rise to liability under

Part I. Section 5(1) states "Subject to the following provisions of this section, in this Part "damage" means death or personal injury or any loss of or damage to any property (including land)". Thus it covers:

(a) *death:* s.6 makes it clear that both the Law Reform (Miscellaneous Provisions) Act 1934 and the Fatal Accidents Act 1976 apply to liability under Part I;
(b) *personal injury:* s.45 provides that this "includes any disease and any other impairment of a person's physical or mental condition". As s.6(3) applies the Congenital Disabilities (Civil Liability) Act 1976 to Part I, it also includes pre-natal injury;
(c) loss of any property (including land);
(d) damage to any property (including land).

In cases of personal injury and death, the damages recoverable under Part I are the same as in other personal injury and fatal cases. They consist of general damages for pain, suffering and loss of amenities together with damages for financial loss consequent on the injury or death. In cases of loss or damage to property, however, Part I creates three distinctive rules of its own which are set out in s.5(2) - (4).

Section 5(2) states that:

"A person shall not be liable under section 2 above in respect of any defect in a product for the loss of or any damage to the product itself or for the loss of or any damage to the whole or any part of any product which has been supplied with the product in question comprised in it".

Thus claims for loss of or damage to the defective product itself or its components are excluded under Part I. If a newly bought television explodes due to an electric fault, causing injury to its owner, damaging his furniture, and destroying itself in the process, he may recover damages under Part I for his injuries and the damage to his furniture, but not for the destruction of the television. Consequently claims for loss of or damage to the defective product itself must continue to be based in contract or tort. The rationale of this has been stated as follows:

"Liability in respect of the quality of a product, its fitness for a particular purpose, including its freedom from defects in the sense that it will not be damaged or lost in its entirety as a result of defects in part of it, is normally governed in the laws of all the member States by the law relating to the sale of goods".

In the UK, the main provisions are contained in the Sale of Goods Act 1979.

The rule applies not only to the defective product itself but also to the loss of or damage to any product which has been supplied with the defective product comprised in it. Suppose that a new motor car is sold with a defective battery which malfunctions and burns out the car. Section 5(2) does not only debar the owner from recovering under Part I for damage to the battery. It also prevents him from recovering for the loss of the whole car which has been supplied with the defective battery comprised in it.

Consequently it is critically important whether a defective component has been supplied as part of the main product. If a car is supplied with a component and the component fails, s.5(2) applies because the component has been supplied with the car. If the component fails, is replaced subsequently and the replacement fails, s.5(2) does not apply because the replacement has not been supplied with the vehicle. This was accepted on behalf of the government by Lord Cameron of Lochbroom who illustrated it with the following example:

"For instance, a manufacturer may supply a car with a defective radio in it and the radio may cause the car to be destroyed. So far as the Directive is concerned, there is no claim against the car manufacturer for the product which he has supplied. That has always been clear. Neither is there a claim under the Directive against the manufacturer of the radio in the car in which it was a component. If a similar defective radio were bought by a consumer and subsequently installed in an identical motor car and the radio destroyed the motor car, there would be different consequences. In that case the radio in the car would be regarded as a different product under the Directive and, although one would not be able to claim for damage to the defective radio, one would be able in that case to claim for damage to the car".

Part I's second distinctive rule about lost or damaged property is contained in s.5(3):

"A person shall not be liable under section 2 above for any loss of or damage to any property which, at the time it is lost or damaged, is not -
(a) of a description of property ordinarily intended for private use, occupation or consumption; and
(b) intended by the person suffering the loss or damage mainly for his own private use, occupation or consumption".

The word "intended" is used to cover cases where property is damaged before as well as after it is put into use. The word "private" is used to indicate the activities of the victim outside his occupation(s) or profession(s). Therefore, while Part I protects private property, damage to commercial property is not covered. The criteria are a combination of the objective ("ordinarily intended") and the subjective ("intended by the person suffering").

Application of the objective criterion obviously excludes loss of or damage to heavy goods vehicles, cranes and other industrial equipment. Often, however, the subjective criterion will be decisive. Loss of a private car is covered by Part I of the Act, but damage to a *bona fide* company car is not. If the house in which the victim lives is blown up by a defective product, the damage to it is covered by Part I, but not if he is renting it out as a landlord. The context of the loss or damage usually manifests the intention. If fire in an owner's house damages his washing machine, he can claim for this damage under Part I. If fire in a hospital damages a washing machine used to wash sheets and towels, this damage is not recoverable under Part I although, as the exception only applies to property, this would not prevent patients, hospital staff or anyone else from claiming damages for their injuries.

Part I's third distinctive rule on lost or damaged property is found in s.5(4):

> "No damages shall be awarded to any person by virtue of this Part in respect of any loss of or damage to any property if the amount which would fall to be so awarded to that person, apart from this subsection and any liability for interest, does not exceed £275".

This appears to contemplate that the total value of the claim may be higher than £275, and to concentrate on the net figure after any deduction for contributory negligence. The rule is also to be applied before interest is added. Suppose that the value of a painting damaged beyond repair is £500 and that the owner is guilty of 50% contributory negligence. This reduces his damages to £250. The addition of £50 interest brings his claim up to £300. Section 5(4) prevents him from recovering damages for the painting under Part I because the amount that would fall to be awarded to him apart from interest is only £250. The purpose of the rule is to discourage small claims for property loss or damage, which thus can only be brought under the existing law.

The Act's special rules in relation to property loss or damage may be summarised as follows. No compensation is recoverable under Part I in respect of any loss of or damage to:

(a) the defective product itself or any product which has been supplied with the defective product comprised in it (s.5(2));

(b) any property not ordinarily intended or not in fact intended by the victim, for his private use, occupation or consumption (s.5(3));

(c) any property giving rise to damages, in respect of its loss or damage, not exceeding £275 net of interest (s.5(4)).

These exceptions only concern the type of property loss or damage that is recoverable. They do not limit what sort of property can found liability for a claim. Compensation cannot be recovered under the Act in respect of damaged cranes or light bulbs. If such products are defective, however, and cause damage in consequence they give rise to liability under Part I.

Section 5(5) - (7) is relevant in determining who has suffered loss or damage to property and when the loss or damage occurred. This is particularly pertinent in a case where the damage could not initially be discovered. The answer is that it is when any person with an interest in the property had knowledge of such facts as would lead a reasonable person with such an interest to consider the loss or damage sufficiently serious to justify his instituting proceedings for damages against a defendant who did not dispute liability and was able to satisfy a judgment. In view of s.5(4), this cannot be until he knows facts showing that the value of the loss or damage to the property exceeds £275. Knowledge for this purpose includes knowledge which a person might reasonably have been expected to acquire from facts observable by him, or from facts ascertainable by him (with the help of any appropriate expert advice which it is reasonable for him to seek).

6. Claimants

Part I does not explicitly define who may claim under it. There is no need, because there is no limitation. It is not necessary for the victim to have entered into a contract to buy the defective product. Nor is it necessary for him to be within the range of people to whom duties are owed under the traditional torts. He need not be the owner of the defective product. He need not even have been using it. He may have been injured as a consumer, an employee, a passer-by, a resident, a passenger, a client, a visitor or even a trespasser. It matters not which.

The only qualification is that he must have suffered damage within the meaning of s.5. As seen above, this excludes claims in respect of commercial property. It also excludes claims for pure economic loss. Part I is designed to compensate individuals rather than companies.

Section 6 provides for fatal and pre-natal injuries. Section 6(1) applies the Fatal Accidents Act 1976 to claims under Part I. Section 6(2) confirms that the Law Reform (Miscellaneous Provisions) Act 1934 is also applied. Section 6(3) applies the Congenital Disabilities (Civil Liability) Act 1976. Thus claims under Part I for death due to defective products are to be pursued as in other fatal cases. And a person is entitled to claim in respect of pre-natal injury caused by a defective product.

Chapter 3

Defences under the new Act

Article 4 of the EC Directive states that "The injured person shall be required to prove the damage, the defect and the causal relationship between defect and damage". This is not reproduced in Part I because, as far as UK law is concerned, it is automatic. The burden of proof rests on the injured person who must discharge it on the balance of probabilities.

Defences to a claim under Part I are divisible into four main categories:

(a) the injured person has been unable to discharge the burden of proof, ie he has not been able to show that his claim falls within Part I;

(b) the defendant is able to establish one of the specified defences in s.4 of the Act;

(c) the claimant is debarred from proceeding by one or more of the Act's time limits;

(d) the defences of contributory negligence or *volenti non fit injuria* apply.

This chapter will consider each category in turn.

1. Claim not within the Act

An injured person might be unable to establish within the meaning of Part I:

- a product;
- that his chosen defendant(s) is(are) liable;
- a defect;

- damage;
- that the defect caused the damage.

Thus there are five defences to the effect that Part I has no application in a particular case.

Product

The Act's definition of product, set out in s.1(2), has been discussed in Chapter 2. Briefly, a defect does not give rise to liability under Part I if it is:

(a) an item which has not been industrially produced, eg natural flowers;

(b) immovable property, eg land and buildings;

(c) incidental waste, eg effluent from a factory;

(d) primary agricultural produce, eg raw fish or fruit.

Defendants

Part I's range of defendants, set out in s.2, has also been considered in Chapter 2. Depending on the facts, possible defences for a person sued are:

(a) that he did not produce the product; someone else did;

(b) although he was the producer of a component within the defective product, he was not the producer of the defective component;

(c) although a processor of the product, he was not its producer because his processing did not alter its essential characteristics;

(d) although he branded the product with his name or other distinguishing mark, he did not hold himself out to be its producer;

(e) although he imported the product into the UK, he did not import it from outside the EC; either someone else did, or it was produced within the EC.

(f) as a supplier:
  - the injured person's request for identification was not made within a reasonable period after the damage occurred;

- the request was not made by the injured person;
- it was reasonably practicable for the person making the request to identify all those whose identity he was seeking;
- although he did not comply with the request, he identified the person who supplied the product to him;
- he is not required to identify the producer of a defective component in a finished product.

Defect

The definition of defect, set out in s.3, has been discussed in Chapter 2. There is no defect if:

(a) the product is perfectly safe;
(b) the product is as safe as persons generally are entitled to expect, in view of its nature and presentation;
(c) the damage only arose through the disregard of instructions or warnings;
(d) the damage only arose because the product was put to an unexpected use;
(e) the damage was solely caused by fair wear and tear;
(f) knowledge that the product could be made more safe only became available after its producer supplied it.

The question of whether there is a defect involves what is sometimes termed "state of the art" evidence. This term is employed in two main ways. First, to consider what level of safety people are entitled to expect. Second, to support a "development risks" defence. In its first use, it is devoted to the issue of whether a defect exists at all. The development risks defence, in contrast, only arises when there is a defect, as in thalidomide products, but "state of the art" evidence is invoked to argue that this defect could not have been known at the relevant time.

Damage

The definition of damage in s.5 has also been considered in Chapter 2. There is no damage within the meaning of Part I if the damage consists of:

(a) pure economic loss;
(b) loss of or damage to the defective product itself or any product which has been supplied with the defective product comprised in it;
(c) loss of or damage to commercial property;
(d) loss of or damage to any property, which loss or damage does not give rise to damages exceeding £275 net of interest.

Causation

The injured person must prove the causal relationship between defect and damage. Section 2(1) creates strict liability where any damage is caused "wholly or partly" by a defect in the product. Thus it is not necessary to prove that the defect was solely responsible for the damage, but only that it was partly responsible.

The burden of proof lies with the victim. He must discharge it on the balance of probabilities. Thus he has to establish that the defect was probably at least partly responsible for his damage. Assistance may in some cases be derived from the House of Lords decision in *McGhee v National Coal Board* (1973) in which it was held that, when the precise cause of an injury is unknown, but the defendant's fault has materially increased the risks of that injury, then the defendant is deemed to have caused it. The principle may be invoked, for example, in drug damage cases. Subject to this:

(a) there is a complete defence if the victim cannot prove that any of his damage was probably caused by a defect in the product;
(b) damages will be reduced, in so far as the victim cannot prove that some part of his damage was caused by the defect, eg if he can prove that it bruised his head, but not that it was responsible for his subsequent epilepsy.

2. Section 4 defences

Section 4(1) of the Act states that:

> "In any civil proceedings by virtue of this Part against any person ("the person proceeded against") in respect of a defect in a product it shall be a defence for him to show -"

any one of six sets of facts, eg the development risks defence.

These six defences are different in two important ways from the five defences discussed above. They only arise when the victim has established a *prima facie* claim under Part I; and the burden of proof is on the defendant to establish them.

Compliance with requirements (s.4(1)(a))

It shall be a defence for the defendant to show:

> "that the defect is attributable to compliance with any requirement imposed by or under any enactment or with any Community obligation".

This defence is strictly defined and will rarely arise in practice. Requirements imposed "by or under any enactment" include statutory regulations as well as Acts. The requirement must be mandatory; compliance with British Standards or the like does not invoke the defence. Moreover the defect must be due to the compliance; if it merely accompanies compliance, it is outside the scope of the defence. It is the very fact of compliance that must make the product defective. An example is where national or EC law requires a product to contain a certain substance, presumably in the interests of safety, and that substance is later realised to have rendered the product defective. This is not inconceivable. Asbestos, for instance, was admired for its fireproofing value long before its carcinogenic qualities became known.

Non-supply (s.4(1)(b))

It is a defence for the defendant to show "that the person proceeded against did not at any time supply the product to another".

Part I is directed at the supply of defective products. Thus liability is excluded in respect of, for example:

- stolen products;
- prototypes;
- pharmaceuticals used for clinical tests before any supply;
- products for the producer's own use, such as lifting tackle for his factory;
- products which cause injury through their own production process.

The two latter examples will generally be governed by such statutes as the Factories Act 1961 and the Employers Liability (Defective Equipment) Act 1969.

Non-business transaction (s.4(1)(c))

It shall be a defence for the defendant to show:

"that the following conditions are satisfied, that is to say -
(i) that the only supply of the product to another by the person proceeded against was otherwise than in the course of a business of that person's; and
(ii) that section 2(2) above does not apply to that person or applies to him by virtue only of things done otherwise than with a view to profit".

It was stated above that Part I is directed at the supply of defective products. This defence demonstrates that it is aimed at their business supply. Amateur and most private transactions are exempt. The Law Commission has furnished the following examples:

"A housewife, for instance, who makes home-made jam

for her local church ...... should not be liable; nor should the man who sells apples to his neighbour over the garden wall. On the other hand, the country dweller who provides home-made teas for tourists throughout the summer, and the small-scale market gardener, would presumably be regarded as acting in the course of business".

Relevant time (s.4(1)(d))

It shall be a defence for the defendant to show "that the defect did not exist in the product at the relevant time". This is an important defence that is likely to arise far more often in practice than the more famous development risks defence.

Section 4(2) states that:

"In this section 'the relevant time', in relation to electricity, means the time at which it was generated, being a time before it was transmitted or distributed, and in relation to any other product, means -
(a) if the person proceeded against is a person to whom subsection (2) of section 2 above applies in relation to the product, the time when he supplied the product to another;
(b) if that subsection does not apply to that person in relation to the product, the time when the product was last supplied by a person to whom that subsection does apply in relation to the product."

This confirms that Part I only applies to defects when electricity is generated (ie produced), not when it is later supplied, eg to the Central Electricity Generating Board, rather than to the local electricity boards who distribute electricity.

More generally, the producer, own-brander or EC importer will not be liable if he proves that the defect did not exist when he supplied the product. If the producer of a defective component is sued, the relevant time is when the component part itself is supplied. So far as the liability of a distributor or retailer under s.2(3) is concerned, the relevant time is not when he supplied the product, nor necessarily when he received it, but when it was last supplied by a s.2(2) defendant.

Suppose that in February Pr produces a safari tent in Kenya. In March he supplies it to Im who imports it into the EC. In April Im supplies it to Wh. In May Wh supplies it to Re. In June Re sells it to Mr V who is injured. If Pr is sued, the relevant time is March. If Im, Wh or Re is sued, the relevant time is April.

The defence under s.4(1)(d) is particularly important for products with a short life expectancy or which are known to be damaged by wear and tear or lack of repair. It also applies to products accompanied by warnings and instructions which are detached by an intermediary and to goods which are damaged through not being stored correctly. The defence also covers deliberate tampering, as when poison is maliciously inserted into food products in order to attack the producer's reputation.

The older the product, the higher the chance that the defect has arisen since supply. Many are the dangerous old bangers roaming the roads that were perfectly safe when first supplied brand new by their producers. It follows that many defective old and second-hand products are outside the scope of Part I. Those injured by them will have to rely on the existing laws of contract and tort.

Development risks (s.4(1)(e))

It shall be a defence for the defendant to show:

> "that the state of scientific and technical knowledge at the relevant time was not such that a producer of products of the same description as the product in question might be expected to have discovered the defect if it had existed in his products while they were under his control."

This is known as the development risks defence.

As seen above, the relevant time is when the product is supplied, not when it is manufactured. Thus the defence does not apply if the producer might be expected to have discovered the defect by the time of supply, even if there was no reason for him to know of it when the product was made. If sufficient new information becomes available between the time of manufacture and the time of supply, the producer is expected to act on it.

Moreover the relevant time is not when the type of product was first supplied, but when the particular product itself was supplied. Thus the defence is not a licence to continue to distribute products realised to be defective merely because at the time of their initial supply the type of product was thought to be safe.

The reference to "a producer of products of the same description as the product in question" raises the question of a sole producer or a unique product. If someone is the only producer of a product, for instance if he has the patent on it, is he the only person who is expected to have discovered the defect? Similarly, what is the position if injury is caused by a one-off product and there are no other products of the same description? Lord Lucas of Chilworth answered on behalf of the government:

> "...... the only plausible interpretation must be that the information which is available is such that any reasonable person, looking at the matter in an objective way, would say that the producer should carry out such-and-such investigations or should carry out such-and-such tests ...... The noble Lord, Lord Allen, asked me about the producer of a unique product. That is quite easy if one considers what a hypothetical producer of products of that type would be expected to know and do."

The above answer invokes traditional principles of the tort of negligence. Mr M Howard, Parliamentary Under-Secretary of State for Trade and Industry, spoke in similar terms when discussing the problem of remote or speculative information:

"Let us suppose, for example, that there has been a speculative account, perhaps in an obscure academic journal, which just might bear upon the potential effects of a given product. Does that mean that the practical implications must be thought through and tested by any producer of that product before he can properly put that product on the market ...... it is not what the Directive intends. The only plausible interpretation of the Directive is that the information to be taken into account is that which any reasonable objective person would say a producer of products of that kind should be expected to act upon".

Whether or not the Minister is correct in his interpretation of the Directive, there can be little doubt as to what the Act has achieved. So far as discovery of a defect is concerned, s.4(1)(e) effectively preserves the principles of negligence law. Only the onus of proof is different. Once a defect is or might be expected to have been discovered, however, the strict liability of s.2(1) applies. The producer cannot plead how difficult or expensive it would have been to have eliminated the defect. If he ought to have discovered it, it will not assist him to show that he manufactured the product to an accepted national or international safety standard. Nor can he rely on traditional practice by others in his industry. Moreover the defence by its nature principally applies to advanced technological industries such as aerospace and pharmaceuticals. It ought not to exclude liability for defects in the majority of routine and standard products like motor cycles and washing machines.

Nevertheless the inclusion of the defence has left a significant gap in the network of strict product liability. The rationale is that otherwise industrial innovation would be inhibited and technological progress impeded. The result is that, while the difficulty experienced by the thalidomide claimants in seeking compensation was one of the mainsprings leading to the Directive and the Act, those injured in similar circumstances may go uncompensated in future. It has been decided in the UK that this is a price which has to be paid.

The defence as finally worded above represents the outcome of a legislative tug-of-war. Article 7(e) of the Directive states that the defence should apply if the producer proves "that the state of scientific and technical knowledge at the time when he put the product into circulation was not such as to enable the existence of the defect to be discovered." This is more tightly and narrowly drawn than the wording in s.4(1)(e) of the Act, so much so that it is questionable whether the Act accurately complies with the Directive in this respect. The wording in s.4(1)(e) was inserted in the initial draft Bill presented to the House of Lords. During the Report stage in the Lords, an amendment was carried that restored the original wording in the Directive. Then in the Committee stage in the House of Commons the government succeeded in reinserting the final form of wording.

Article 15(1)(b) of the Directive provides that each member State may opt to exclude the defence from its national legislation. It is understood that France, Belgium and Luxembourg intend to do so and that West Germany will not permit the defence in cases involving pharmaceutical products. Many of the other EC States are expected to include the defence in the terms of the Directive. Then there is a third category, of which the UK is founder member, recasting the defence according to its own national concept of it.

Article 15(3) provides that ten years after the Directive, that is in 1995, the EC Commission shall report on the operation of the development risks defence and that the EC Council of Ministers will then decide whether to repeal it.

Component producer (s.4(1)(f))

It shall be a defence for the defendant to show:

"that the defect -
(i) constituted a defect in a product ("the subsequent product") in which the product in question had been comprised; and
(ii) was wholly attributable to the design of the subsequent

product or to compliance by the producer of the product in question with instructions given by the producer of the subsequent product".

This is the component producer's defence. As seen above, "products" include components and producers of components are liable for defects in them. The defence contemplates the situation where component parts, such as nuts and bolts, are made to the order of the finished product manufacturer, who then uses them for purposes for which they were not designed. The defence exculpates the component producer, once his component has been comprised in the subsequent product, in two circumstances. First, if the defect was wholly (not partly) attributable to the design of the final product. Second, if the defect was wholly (not partly) attributable to the component producer's compliance with instructions. The instructions must be those given to the component producer, not to the consumer. Moreover they must be given by the producer of the subsequent product, who can be sued in his own right. The defence does not cover replacement components produced in accordance with a retailer's instructions.

The defence does not protect producers of building materials, since the buildings in which they are comprised are not products within the meaning of Part I.

If the component producer knows of the defect, this does not appear to destroy his defence. Nevertheless, he could be liable in negligence, if he makes a component to a specification which he knows would result in danger once it is comprised in the final product.

3. Time limit defences

There are three main time defences. First, s.50(7) of the Act excludes liability in respect of any product supplied by its producer before the coming into force of Part I. In addition, Schedule 1 to the Act lays down two main limitation periods:

(a) ten years from the relevant time of supply of the

product;

(b) within the ten year period, three years from whichever is the later of the date on which the cause of action accrued or the date of the injured person's knowledge of material facts.

Section 50

Section 50(7) states:

"Nothing in this Act ...... shall make any person liable by virtue of Part I of this Act for any damage caused wholly or partly by a defect in a product which was supplied to any person by its producer before the coming into force of Part I of this Act."

The important point is the supply of the product by its producer to any person. "Producer", as throughout Part I, is used in its strict sense whereby it literally means the producer. It does not loosely cover an own-brander or importer as well. It is the supply by the producer that counts for this purpose, not any later supply to the consumer. Thus if a product is made in 1986, supplied by its producer to a EC importer in May 1987, supplied by the EC importer to an English retailer in August 1988 and sold to the consumer in November 1988, the Act does not apply because the producer supplied the product in May 1987 before it came into force.

Section 50(7) refers to the particular defective product, not to the type or line of product. Thus while the Act does not operate retrospectively, so far as the particular product is concerned, it can affect established lines of products, if defective products in that line are supplied by their producer after Part I comes into force.

Liability life

Section 6(6) and Schedule 1 of the Act insert s.11A into the Limitation Act 1980:

"11A - (1)   This section shall apply to an action for damages by virtue of any provision of Part I of the Consumer Protection Act 1987.

(2) None of the time limits given in the preceding provisions of this Act shall apply to an action to which this section applies.

(3) An action to which this section applies shall not be brought after the expiration of ten years from the relevant time, within the meaning of section 4 of the said Act of 1987; and this subsection shall operate to extinguish a right of action and shall do so whether or not that right of action had accrued, or time under the following provisions of this Act had begun to run, at the end of the said period of ten years".

Thus s.11A(3) creates the concept of a liability life of ten years. "The relevant time" is defined in s.4(2) and has been considered in this chapter under the s.4(1)(d) defence. Excluding electricity, it means:

"(a) if the person proceeded against is a person to whom subsection (2) of section 2 above applies in relation to the product, the time when he supplied the product to another;

(b) if that subsection does not apply to that person in relation to the product, the time when the product was last supplied by a person to whom that subsection does apply in relation to the product".

The combined effect of these sections is illustrated by the following example. In October 1987 Pr produces the product. In September 1988 he supplies it to Im. In November 1988 Im imports it into the EC. In December 1988 Im supplies it to OB. In January 1989 OB puts his name on the product and hold himself out as its producer. In February 1989 OB sells the product to Mr CV. In March 1989 Mrs CV is injured by a defect in the product.

If Pr is to be sued, the relevant time is September 1988. If Im is to be sued, the relevant time is December 1988. If OB is to be sued, the relevant time is February 1989. Had Im supplied the product to a pure retailer Re instead of to OB, the relevant time for Re would be December 1988. It follows that the longstop ten year period laid down by s.11A(3) expires against different parties at different times. In the example, these will be between September 1998 and February 1999.

For a component producer, the relevant time is when he supplied the component. If he supplied it in 1988, it matters not that it may not be incorporated into the final product until 1991 or that the final product may not be supplied by its producer until 1993, or still less that it is resold in 1996. The ten year period expires against the component producer in 1998.

This ten year longstop limitation period is absolute. It applies even if the victim does not learn of the defect, and even if he is not injured by it, until after the ten years have expired. Thus persons injured by products with latent defects which do not appear, or which do not cause injury, for at least ten years will not be able to claim under Part I. The ten year period overrides any other limitation period or rule that conflicts with it, eg in the Limitation Act 1980, s.28 (extension of limitation period in case of disability); s.32 (postponement of limitation period in case of fraud, concealment or mistake); and s.33 (discretionary exclusion of time limit).

It follows that those who suffer injury, loss or damage due to a defective product close to the end of the ten year period must sue quickly if they are to recover under Part I at all. A victim injured after nine and a half years will have only six months left. Those who cannot or do not commence court action within the ten year period must rely on the existing laws of contract and tort and the limitation periods applicable to them.

Three year limitation

In addition to the ten year longstop period above, the Act provides a primary three year limitation period. Section

11A(4) states:

"Subject to subsection (5) below, an action to which this section applies in which the damages claimed by the plaintiff consist of or include damages in respect of personal injuries to the plaintiff or any other person or loss of or damage to any property, shall not be brought after the expiration of the period of three years from whichever is the later of:

(a) the date on which the cause of action accrued; and
(b) the date of knowledge of the injured person or, in the case of loss of or damage to property, the date of knowledge of the plaintiff or (if earlier) of any person in whom his cause of action was previously vested".

The date on which the cause of action accrued is the date of the accident or, if different, the date on which injury was first sustained due to the defect. Section 14(1A) provides for the purpose of the Act that a person's date of knowledge is the date on which he first knew:

(a) such facts about the damage caused by the defect as would lead a reasonable person to consider it sufficiently serious to justify his instituting proceedings; and
(b) that the damage was wholly or partly attributable to the defect; and
(c) the identity of the defendant.

It is irrelevant whether he knew he had a valid claim in law. In property damage cases, any knowledge he had before he acquired a right of action (eg before he became the owner) is to be disregarded.

Section 11A(5)-(13) of the Limitation Act 1980 apply Part I to fatal cases. In brief, the primary limitation period is three years from the date of injury or death or, if later, three years from the date of knowledge of certain material facts. Often there will be no difference; for instance, if defective food is sold by an own-brander and causes injury as soon as it is eaten. In other cases, the date of knowledge will succeed the date of the injury: for example, the causal relationship between injury and a defective drug may not be immediately apparent, or it may reasonably take time for the victim of an anonymous defective product to learn the identity of its producer.

There are important differences between the primary three year limitation period and the ten year longstop period. The three year period is victim orientated, in that it concentrates on the date of injury or the injured person's knowledge, whereas the ten year period is defendant orientated, in that it is defined by reference to the date of supply by the producer, own-brander or EC importer. Also, the ten year period is absolute, whereas within this ten year period the three year period may be extended in cases of disability, fraud, concealment or mistake or, by s.33 of the Limitation Act 1980, in the discretion of the court when it thinks it equitable to do so.

4. Contributory negligence and volenti non fit injuria

Section 6(4) applies the Law Reform (Contributory Negligence) Act 1945, thereby allowing the defence of contributory negligence. Also it is implicit in the wording of Part I that the defence of *volenti non fit injuria* may be raised.

Contributory negligence

Section 6(4) of the Act states:

"Where any damage is caused partly by a defect in a product and partly by the fault of the person suffering the damage, the Law Reform (Contributory Negligence) Act 1945 and section 5 of the Fatal Accidents Act 1976 (contributory negligence) shall have effect as if the defect were the fault of every person liable by virtue of this Part for the damage caused by the defect".

Thus contributory negligence is a defence to claims under Part I. While it is not necessary for the victim to prove fault against the producer or other defendant in order to recover damages under Part I, the defendant must prove fault on the part of the victim if those damages are to be reduced. Usually a defence of contributory negligence, if upheld, leads to a proportionate reduction, ie a victim who is 25% to blame for his accident recovers 75% of his damages. In extreme cases, however, the victim's contributory negligence may amount to 100%, in which event he will recover nothing.

Examples of contributory negligence in product liability cases include:

- failing to follow instructions or heed warnings;
- ignoring obvious dangers;
- failing to respond to a recall letter;
- carelessly handling or damaging the product;
- storing it in bad conditions;
- keeping food or drink too long;
- failing to have a car properly maintained and serviced;
- using the product after a defect became apparent.

The list, which is far from exhaustive, assumes a defect in the product. On occasions, however, a victim's negligence may be so profound as to call into question the very existence of a defect, for instance, when a product which might otherwise have been safe is put to a totally unreasonable use.

Volenti non fit injuria

No injury is done to one who consents. One who consents to injury cannot be heard to complain of it thereafter. However this Latin maxim is translated or explained, the defence has two elements. First, the claimant agreeing to the defendant's breach of duty towards him. Second, his waiving his right of action arising out of such breach. Both are normally necessary. Lord Denning stated in *Nettleship* v *Weston* (1971): "Knowledge of the risk of injury is not enough. Nor is a willingness to take the risk of injury. Nothing will suffice short of an agreement to waive any claim for negligence."

This general defence is not mentioned in Part I. Yet it is apparent that it is applicable. Often it is intertwined with the issue of whether there is a defect. If necessary, it could be raised as a defence by cigarette producers. They might not need to do so, however, since a product is only defective if its safety is not such as persons generally are entitled to expect; and the risk of lung cancer from smoking is so well known that it is hard to argue cigarettes are defective just because they cause it.

The purer application of the defence arises when there is a defect but the victim accepts this and, if only by implication, consents to waive any right of action arising from it. If someone playing Russian roulette shoots himself, the gun is not defective and the defence is not needed. If, in contrast, the gun has a faulty safety catch which he is aware is apt to malfunction, and after pointing the gun at himself with the safety catch on he pulls the trigger, the defence applies if the gun goes off.

Volenti non fit injuria is a total defence; if it is established, the victim recovers no damages. Thus it is to be contrasted with the defence of contributory negligence, which usually operates as a partial defence to reduce damages.

5. Disclaimers ineffective

Section 7 of the Act rules out a possible defence. It states:

> "The liability of a person by virtue of this Part to a person who has suffered damage caused wholly or partly by a defect in a product, or to a dependant or relative of such a person, shall not be limited or excluded by any contract term, by any notice or by any other provision".

Suppose that Pr produces a motor cycle and supplies it to Re with a leaflet in which Pr disclaims any liability for personal injury or property damage arising out of the motor cycle's use. Re sells the motor cycle to Mr V and passes on the leaflet. While Mr V is riding the motor cycle, it crashes due to a defect in it. In consequence, his expensive clothing is damaged beyond repair. The disclaimer in the leaflet is ineffective. Mr V can recover damages against Pr.

This is more sweeping than the Unfair Contract Terms Act 1977. There is no need to prove that the the contract term or notice is unfair. Nor is any distinction drawn between personal injury and property damage cases. It is impossible to limit or exclude liability to meet victims' claims under the Act.

Nevertheless, it is still possible for businesses to allocate liability amongst themselves by means of contract terms and exclusion clauses. The Unfair Contract Terms Act 1977 continues to apply to these.

6. Conclusion

Part I of the Act imposes strict liability on producers and other defendants. There is no need for the claimant to prove fault on their part. Indeed they may be innocent of any real responsibility for the defect. This has led many in industry to express concern that they might in effect end up as insurers of products, responsible for any injury or loss resulting from their use, and confronted by a virtual *carte blanche* for claimants to recover damages regardless of the circumstances.

However, according to the classification adopted in this chapter, there is a total of sixteen possible defences. This abundance demonstrates that Part I has not imposed absolute product liability. There will still be cases of victims suffering damage from products, even indisputably defective products, who will be unable to recover compensation. Therefore Part I has strengthened without perfecting the overall position of the victims of defective products. More will recover damages than before, but not all.

Chapter 4

The effects of the new law: case studies

This chapter takes eight cases concluded under the old law; they have not been mentioned earlier in this book. After showing how each was decided, it seeks to suggest what result would now be reached under Part I of the Act. This is intended to illustrate how Part I may affect the outcome of product liability claims.

Each case is divided into four parts. "Facts" sets out the facts. "Existing law" records the conclusion reached under the traditional laws of contract and tort. "Part I" indicates the application of the new law through Part I of the Act. "Differences" draws distinctions between the two. As the traditional laws of contract and tort remain in force, the remedies under "Existing law" are to be added to those provided by "Part I". The old law and the new law supplement each other; they are not mutually exclusive alternatives.

1. Daniels & Daniels v R White & Sons Ltd & Tarbard (1938)

Facts

One July evening, Mr Daniels entered the Falcon Arms public house in Battersea. He bought from Mrs Tarbard, the licensee, a bottle of R White's lemonade, which was made and bottled by R White & Sons Ltd. He also purchased from her a jug of beer. He took both the jug of beer and the bottle of lemonade home. On arrival, Mr Daniels opened the bottle and poured a little lemonade into the jug of beer. He also poured some of the lemonade into a glass, which his wife then immediately drank, and he drank some lemonade too. Both Mr and Mrs Daniels drank the lemonade almost simultaneously, and they both immediately realised that there was something burning in the liquid that they had taken, and they at once thought that they had been poisoned. It was discovered that the bottle of lemonade contained 38 grains of carbolic acid.

Existing law

Mr Daniels sued Mrs Tarbard for breach of contract. His wife could not do so, because she did not buy the lemonade. Both Mr and Mrs Daniels also sued Whites for negligence. Whites gave evidence of an extensive system of bottling and supervision. It was held that Mrs Tarbard was liable to Mr Daniels for his injuries under s.14(2) of the Sale of Goods Act 1893. It was further held that Whites were not negligent, so there was judgment in favour of Whites against Mr and Mrs Daniels.

Part I

The lemonade is defective: s.3(1). Mr and Mrs Daniels suffered damage: s.5(1). There is strict liability for this: s.2(1). It rests with Whites, the producer: s.2(2)(a). Mr and Mrs Daniels can recover damages from Whites under Part I. This is without prejudice to Mr Daniels' right to sue Mrs Tarbard in contract: s.2(6).

Differences

Two main differences result from the application of Part I. First, it is unnecessary to prove negligence against Whites. Second, Mrs Daniels, as well as her husband, can recover damages.

2. Jackson v Watson & Sons (1909)

Facts

Mr Jackson bought tinned salmon from Watson & Sons, grocers and provision merchants. He and his wife both ate the salmon. It was unfit for human consumption. In consequence, he became ill and she died. He sued Watson & Sons for breach of contract and negligence.

Existing law

It was held that Watson & Sons were in breach of their implied warranty under s.14(1) of the Sale of Goods Act 1893 that the salmon was fit for human food. There was no evidence of negligence and this allegation was not pursued. While Mr Jackson could recover damages for his own losses, there could have been no claim on behalf of his wife's estate (even if the law of the day had allowed it), because she was not a party to the contract for the purchase of the tinned salmon.

Part I

The tinned salmon is defective: s.3(1). Strict liability applies: s.2(1). Jackson should if necessary request Watson & Sons to identify the producer of the tinned salmon or their own supplier; if they cannot do either, they are liable themselves: s.2(3). The salmon is agricultural produce: s.1(2). The processor who tinned it is its producer: s.1(2)(c). If identified, he is liable: s.2(2)(a). Neither s.2(2) nor s.2(3) applies to the fisherman who caught the salmon and initially supplied it, because at that time the salmon had not undergone an industrial process: s.2(4). Accordingly the fisherman is not liable: s.2(2); and Watson & Sons need not identify him: s.2(3). The producer of the tinned salmon is liable to pay full damages: s.2(5). This is without prejudice to his rights, or the Jacksons' rights, to recover from the fisherman in negligence: s.2(6).

Mr Jackson can sue under the Fatal Accidents Act in respect

of Mrs Jackson's death: s.6(1). An action can also be brought on behalf of her estate under the Law Reform (Miscellaneous Provisions) Act 1934. Even if not injured himself, Mr Jackson could request Watson & Sons to identify the producer of the tinned salmon: s.6(2).

Differences

First, without needing to prove negligence, Mr Jackson can recover damages from the producer of the tinned salmon; so can his wife's estate. Second, the potential liability of Watson & Sons is no longer limited to their contract with Mr Jackson; Mrs Jackson's estate (as well as Mr Jackson) can claim against Watson & Sons, if on request they cannot identify within a reasonable period the producer of the tinned salmon or their own supplier.

3. Kasler & Cohen v Slavouski (1928)

Facts

In June 1923 Mr Slavouski (A) sold some dyed rabbit skins to Kasler and Cohen (B) who were wholesale furriers. Kasler and Cohen made them into fur collars for women's coats. They resold to Mace, Rainbow and Stone (C) who resold to Scott, Son & Co (D) who in turn sold to Alexander McMillan (E), a draper who carried on a retail business. McMillan afterwards sold a coat with one of these collars attached to a nurse called Miss White (W). After wearing the collar and coat, she developed dermatitis and sued McMillan for damages for breach of warranty. Her dermatitis was caused by the presence of antimony in the dyed skin which formed the collar of the coat.

Existing law

It was held that E was liable to W under s.14 of the Sale of Goods Act 1893. He recovered these damages and costs from D who recovered them in turn against C who recovered them against B. It was held that B was entitled to recover the damages and costs against A.

Part I

The fur collar and dyed rabbit skins are defective: s.3(1). W suffered damage in the form of personal injury: s.5(1). There is strict liability for this: s.2(1). The fur collar is a product; so are the dyed rabbit skins: s.1(2). If A skinned the rabbits and dyed their skins, he is the producer of the skins: s.1(2)(c). B is the producer of the coat: s.1(2)(a). If identified, A and B are liable: s.2(2)(a). To reach them, W must request E to identify B. He is not required to identify A: s.1(3). Suppose that he is unable to identify B but identifies D. W makes the same request of D. If he is unable to identify B or C, D is liable: s.2(3). If he identifies C who in turn identifies A and B, they pay the damages: s.2(2). Assuming that A subjected the rabbits to an industrial process, he cannot avail himself of the defence for primary game: s.2(4). Either A or B is liable to pay full damages to W: s.2(5).

Thus W proceeds backwards along the chain of supply until she reaches A and B, the producers of the raw material and the finished products. This is without prejudice to her right to sue E under s.14 of the Sale of Goods Act 1979: s.2(6). B should be able to recover an indemnity against A under the Civil Liability (Contribution) Act 1978.

Differences

First, without proving negligence, W is entitled to recover damages against A and B. Second, C or D can be liable, if on request they cannot identify B or their own supplier. Third, E can be liable under Part I (as well as in contract), if on W's request he cannot identify either B or D.

4. Chapelton v Barry UDC (1940)

Facts

On 3 June 1939 David Chapelton went to a beach at Cold Knap, within the area of the Barry Urban District. There was a cafe known as Bindle's Cafe on the beach. Beside

Bindle's cafe there was a pile of deck chairs. By the side of the deck chairs there was a notice that read" Barry Urban District Council, Cold Knap. Hire of chairs 2d. per session of 3 hours". Then followed words to the effect that the public were respectfully requested to obtain tickets for their chairs from the chair attendants, and that these tickets must be retained for inspection. David Chapelton took two chairs from the attendant - one for himself, and one for Miss Andrews who was with him. He received two tickets, glanced at them, and slipped them into his pocket. He had no idea that there were any conditions on the tickets, and he knew nothing about what was on the back of them. He took the chairs to the beach and set them up firmly. When he sat down on one, he went through the canvas and suffered back injury. On the ticket that had been handed to him there appeared the following words: "Available for 3 hours. Time expires where indicated by cut-off and should be retained and shown on request. The Council will not be liable for any accident or damage arising from hire of chair".

Existing law

It was held that the Council were negligent for providing a chair that was unfit for use. It was further held that, in the circumstances, David Chapelton was entitled to assume that all the conditions of hire were contained in the notice near the stack of chairs, so he was not bound by the condition printed on the back of the ticket. Therefore he was entitled to recover damages.

Part I

The deckchair is a product: so is the canvas: s.1(2). Both are defective: s.3(1). Chapelton suffered damage: s.5(1). There is strict liability: s.2(1). In hiring out the deckchair, the Council supplied it: s.46(1)(a). Chapelton should request them to identify its producer: s.2(3). They are not required to identify the producer of the canvas: s.1(3). If the Council cannot identify the producer of the deckchair or their supplier, they are liable: s.2(3). If the producer of the deckchair is identified, he is liable instead; so would be the producer of the canvas: s.2(2)(a). Each has two possible defences. One is that the defect did not exist in the deckchair, or in the canvas, at the respective times of their supply by their producers: s.4(1)(d). The other is that the action was brought more than ten years after the respective times of their supply: s.6(6) inserting s.11A(3) into the Limitation Act 1980. In addition, the producer of the canvas may have the defence that the defect in the deckchair was wholly attributable to its design or to compliance by him with instructions given by the producer of the deckchair: s.4(1)(f). The exclusion term on the ticket is no defence: s.7.

All this is without prejudice to Chapelton's rights to sue the Council in negligence: s.2(6). Under the Unfair Contract Terms Act 1977, they would no longer be able to rely on the condition on the back of the ticket.

Differences

First, without proving negligence, Chapelton can claim damages against the producers of the deckchair and the canvas respectively, if the defect existed at their respective times of supply. Second, each may be able to rely on the ten year limitation long stop period. Third, Chapelton has an additional ground of claim against the Council, if they cannot identify the producer of the deckchair or their own supplier.

5. Wilson and Another v Rickett Cockerell & Co Ltd (1954)

Facts

In June 1951 Mrs Wilson ordered one ton of Coalite on behalf of her husband and herself from Rickett Cockerell & Co Ltd. It was delivered and paid for. In November 1951 she took from the bin some of the material which they had delivered to her and which they thought was Coalite. She made up the fire with it on November 26 at about 7.30 pm, because she and her husband wanted to listen to an item on the wireless which lasted from 7.30 pm until 8.00 pm. Shortly before eight o'clock there was an explosion in the grate. A thick cloud of black smoke came out, the whole basket which held the Coalite shot forward, and most of the Coalite was scattered about the room, some of it falling on Mrs Wilson's dress. Bits of Coalite were found sticking to the wallpaper. The damage cost £117 to put right. Mr and Mrs Wilson were uninjured. They claimed from Rickett & Cockerell & Co Ltd for damage done to the room and furniture.

It was found that the explosion was due to something in the consignment that the defendants delivered. It was not a piece of Coalite itself, but something that came with it, such as a piece of coal, in which was embedded an explosive. The offending piece had not come from the manufacturers of the Coalite, but it had got mixed with it in the course of transit, such as in a coal truck or in a lorry. It was certainly in the consignment before it was delivered to the Wilsons.

Existing law

It was held that neither of the coalmen employed by Rickett Cockerell & Co Ltd was negligent. It was further held that the consignment of Coalite must be considered as a whole and that it was unmerchantable due to the presence in it of the explosive piece. Consequently Mr and Mrs Wilson were entitled to recover damages from Rickett Cockerell under s.14(2) of the Sale of Goods Act 1893.

Part I

The Coalite is a product: s.1(2). It is defective: s.3(1). The Wilsons could ascertain the identity of the producers from Rickett Cockerell: s.2(3). *Prima facie,* there is strict liability (s.2(1)), resting with the producers of the Coalite: s.2(2)(a). However it is a defence for them to show that the explosive was not in the Coalite when they supplied it: s.4(1)(d). Moreover, no damages are to be awarded in respect of the damage to the Wilsons' property, since this only amounted to £117: s.5(4). Accordingly Mr. and Mrs Wilson are not entitled to damages under Part I.

Differences

Mr and Mrs Wilson can recover damages under the existing law but not under the new law. The frequent effect of Part I is to enable victims to sue manufacturers without proving negligence, additionally or alternatively to suing the retailers in contract. In this case, the producers are protected by the defences in ss.4(1)(d) and 5(4).

6. Parker v Oloxo Ltd and Senior (1937)

Facts

Prior to June 1936, Mrs Parker had been in the habit of having her hair treated by Mrs Senior with henna to colour it. Once a fortnight she went to Mrs Senior's shop. The visits were alternately for an application of henna and a shampoo. A fortnight before June 2, Mrs Senior suggested to Mrs Parker that she should have her hair dyed with Oloxo, a liquid dye which Mrs Senior had bought from Oloxo Ltd. Mrs Parker was unwilling to have this dye used on her head, giving as her reason that so many liquid dyes caused skin trouble. She asked if it was safe. Mrs Senior said it was quite safe and perfectly harmless. Mrs Parker said she would think about it and decide before she came back in a fortnight. On June 2 she came back and Mrs Senior asked if she had decided. Mrs Parker again asked if it was safe, and Mrs Senior again assured her that it was. Mrs Parker agreed to have Oloxo applied. The result of the application was that she developed an acute and very painful attack of dermatitis.

Mrs Senior purchased the Oloxo from Oloxo Ltd. The manufacturers were Oloxo Inc in New York. Oloxo Ltd was its English selling company. Their traveller, Leslie Briggs, called on Mrs Senior and told her that the Oloxo was safe. In fact it was dangerous to use without a skin test. Oloxo Ltd required Mrs Senior to address her order to Messrs Watts, hairdressers' sundriesmen.

Existing law

It was held that Mrs Parker was entitled to recover against Mrs Senior in contract and against Oloxo Ltd in tort, and that Mrs Senior was entitled to an indemnity from Oloxo Ltd.

Part I

Whether the hair dye is defective depends on what level of safety persons generally are entitled to expect: s.3(1). In determining this, any instructions or warnings are to be taken into account: s.3(2). The absence of any instructions to carry out a skin test or any warning not to apply the dye without one rendered it defective: s.3. Mrs Parker's disease of dermatitis is a form of personal injury: s.45. So she suffered damage: s.5(1). There is strict liability for this: s.2(1). It rests with Oloxo Inc, the producer of the hair dye (s.2(2)(a)) and with Oloxo Ltd who imported it into the EC from outside: s.2(2)(c). Mrs Senior should have identified Oloxo Ltd to Mrs Parker, who in turn could have ascertained from them the identity of Oloxo Inc: s.2(3). Mrs Parker is entitled to damages against either or both of Oloxo Inc and Oloxo Ltd: s.2(2). If she sues one alone, it must pay the damages in full: s.2(5). This is without prejudice to her right to sue Mrs Senior under s.14 of the Sale of Goods Act 1979: s.2(6).

Differences

Under the existing law, Mrs Parker had to prove negligence in order to recover damages against Oloxo Ltd. This is unnecessary under Part I. In practice, she has no incentive to seek to sue Oloxo Inc, the US company, since she can sue instead Oloxo Ltd, the English company, in its capacity as EC importer.

7. West v Bristol Tramways Company (1908)

Facts

Mr West was a market gardener. Bristol Tramways Company were authorised by the Bristol Tramways Act 1894 to pave certain parts of a road, on which their tramway was laid, with wood paving. Section 8 of this Act provided that "the company shall pave with wood, or by mutual agreement, with other suitable material". Bristol Tramways Company used blocks of soft wood coated with creosote. The fumes given off by the creosote injured plants and shrubs in Mr West's market garden. As an alternative, the company could have used jarrah wood which would not have damaged Mr West's plants and shrubs. There was reason to think that this damage from the creosote fumes was dependent on the time of year the paving was done and that it would not have occurred if the paving operation had been carried out at another time of the year.

Existing law

It was held that, as Bristol Tramways Company did not know that the use of creosoted wood might cause damage, they were not guilty of negligence. However, as the creosote was dangerous, they were liable to Mr West under the principle laid down in *Rylands* v *Fletcher*. The statutory authority was no defence, since Parliament had not authorised the use of creosote.

Part I

Suppose that the blocks of soft wood came coated with creosote. The creosote coated blocks are a product; so is the creosote: s.1(2). Whether they are defective depends on the level of safety that persons generally are entitled to expect: s.3(1). In determining this, there is to be taken into account the presentation of the blocks and any accompanying instructions and warnings (s.3(2)(a)) and what might reasonably be expected to be done with them: s.3(2)(b). The producers of the blocks should have anticipated that they might be used for paving: s.3(2)(b). They should have warned that such paving could only safely be carried out at certain times of the year: s.3(2)(a). If they did not do so, the blocks are defective: s.3(1). It is arguable that the creosote is not defective, on the grounds that persons generally are not

entitled to expect it to be perfectly safe: s.3(1). *Prima facie,*
there is strict liability (s.2(1)) on the producers of the
creosote coated blocks: s.2(2)(a). Mr West can ascertain
their identity from Bristol Tramways Company: s.2(3). The
producers cannot show that the defect is attributable to
compliance with the Bristol Tramways Act, since Bristol
Tramways Company could have complied with this by using
jarrah wood: s.4(1)(a). However, Mr West has not suffered
damage, since his plants and shrubs in his market garden
were not intended for his private use, occupation or
consumption: s.5(3). Therefore he is not entitled to damages
under Part I.

Differences

Under the existing law, Mr West could recover damages
against British Tramways Company. Part I gives him a
prima facie right to sue the producers of the creosote coated
blocks without proving negligence. They are protected by
s.5(3), but it would be otherwise if he had been injured or if
the plants and shrubs had belonged to his private garden.

8. Andrews v Hopkinson (1957)

Facts

George Andrews was a commercial traveller employed on a
house-to-house sale of drapery. He was minded to acquire a
car for private and business purposes. He visited the
premises of Frank Hopkinson who carried on business as a
second-hand car dealer. His son showed Mr Andrews a
small standard 1934 Saloon car and said "It's a good little
bus; I would stake my life on it". He did not expect Mr
Andrews to examine it before use. George Andrews bought
the car on hire-purchase for £120. On 19 September 1952 he
first drove the car himself and made a number of calls. Then
while he was driving on a main road, the car suddenly
swerved towards a lorry and collided with it. Mr Andrews
suffered serious injuries involving the fracture of three ribs
and his left wrist. The car was wrecked. It was found that
the drag link joint of the steering mechanism had failed due to

the badly worn condition of the socket and ball pins.

Existing law

It was held that Hopkinson was liable to Andrews in contract for breach of warranty. It was further held that, as he had sold a car which he ought to have known was dangerous, without any reasonable anticipation that it would be examined by the customer before use, he was also liable in negligence.

Part I

The car is a product; so is the socket and ball pin: s.1(2). They are defective: s.3(1). Andrews could ask Hopkinson to identify the producer of the car: s.2(3) and s.46(2). Hopkinson is not required to identify the producer of the socket and ball pin: s.1(3). It is a defence for the producer of this old car to show that the defect did not exist when he supplied it: s.4(1)(d). It is also a defence for the producer of the socket and ball pin to show that the defect did not exist in the socket and ball pin when he supplied them: s.4(1)(d). It is an absolute defence to the producer of the 1934 car that more than ten years had expired since he supplied it: s.6(6) inserting s.11A(3) into the Limitation Act 1980. This defence is also available to the producer of the socket and ball pin, provided that he had supplied them more than ten years before Andrews started court action: s.6(6). Accordingly Andrews cannot establish liability under Part I.

Were he able to do so, he could recover damages for his personal injuries: s.5(1). However he could not recover damages for the loss of the car. It is not mainly intended for his private use: s.5(3). Moreover, in a claim against the car producer, he would not be able to recover damages in respect of the loss of the defective car itself: s.5(2). In a claim against the producer of the socket and ball pin, he could recover in respect of the loss of the car if the socket and ball pin had been installed later, but not if they were comprised in the car when it was supplied: s.1(2).

Differences

Mr Andrews could recover damages under the existing law, but not under the new law. The car was 18 years old, and Part I does not apply to such aged products. Under the existing law he could recover his full loss, whereas s.5(3) prevents him being awarded damages for loss of the car.

9. Conclusion

This collection of cases demonstrates that the most significant effect of Part I is the way in which it enables claimants to sue producers without proving negligence (*Daniels* v *R White & Sons Ltd*). This grants victims the benefits of strict liability even though they are not privy to any contract; eg Mrs Jackson's estate. In addition, a new form of liability is imposed on own-branders and EC importers: eg Oloxo Ltd. Retailers may indirectly benefit from the increased liability on producers and the other s.2(2) defendants, but they are subject to a new form of liability themselves under s.2(3) if they cannot supply the requested identification (*Kasler and Cohen* v *Slavouski*).

Part I requires a defect to be proved and provides a variety of possible defences (*West* v *British Tramways Company*). It is restrictive in so far as it disallows certain forms of property damage (*Wilson* v *Rickett Cockerell & Co Ltd*). And it does not apply to old products (*Andrews* v *Hopkinson*).

Accordingly the new law contained in Part I is not a panacea that invariably enables product liability claimants to dispense with the existing laws of contract and tort. Instead it needs to be considered in conjunction with contract and the traditional torts. In some cases, it enables claimants to recover damages where they could not have done so before. In many, it adds to their range of remedies. In others, it does not assist them. The era of automatic product liability compensation has still not arrived.

Chapter 5

Forum shopping and risk control

1987 is not only significant for the passing of the Consumer Protection Act. On 1 January 1987 the Civil Jurisdiction and Judgments Act 1982 at last came into force. This implements into UK law the Brussels Convention 1968 designed to govern jurisdiction and enforcement of judgments amongst the EC member States. When these measures are considered in conjunction with the ways in which the EC States have exercised their options under the Directive, the possibilities of "forum shopping" for injured claimants become manifest.

Potential product liability defendants need to be aware of the increased risks of their being held liable in other EC States. Apart from this, they need to plan how to cope with their prospective new liability under UK law. This chapter considers the practical steps open to them and stresses the importance of retaining records. It closes by indicating aspects of company law that may prevent a product victim from recovering damages, even when strict liability applies in his favour.

1. Civil Jurisdiction and Judgments Act 1982

The main purpose of the Civil Jurisdiction and Judgments Act 1982 is to implement the Brussels Convention. The Convention applies to most civil and commercial matters and covers all product liability cases. Section 2(1) of the 1982 Act states that the Convention shall have the force of law in the United Kingdom. At the time of writing, the Convention is operative in only eight of the EC member States - the UK, West Germany, France, Italy, Belgium, the Netherlands,

Luxembourg and Denmark. This chapter will refer to them as "Convention territories".

The Convention confirms that important distinction between *general* jurisdiction and *special* jurisdiction. Article 2 provides for *general* jurisdiction by stating:

> "Subject to the provisions of this Convention, persons domiciled in a Contracting State shall, whatever their nationality, be sued in the courts of that State ...... ".

Thus domicile, not nationality, is the basic ground of jurisdiction. General jurisdiction is possessed by the courts of the defendant's domicile. Article 3 further provides:

> "Persons domiciled in a Contracting State may be sued in the courts of another Contracting State only by virtue of the rules set out in Sections 2 to 6 of this Title ......".

These rules create *special* jurisdiction according to the facts of particular cases. Therefore the first step is to consider where a defendant is domiciled; the courts of that State automatically have general jurisdiction. The second step is to consider whether, in addition, the courts of any other State have special jurisdiction.

A product liability claimant will normally be suing a company. Article 53 states:

> "For the purposes of this Convention, the seat of a company or other legal person or association of natural or legal persons shall be treated as its domicile. However, in order to determine that seat, the court shall apply its rules of private international law......".

Thus Danish courts will apply Danish rules of law to determine whether a Belgian company has its seat in Denmark.

Section 42(3) of the 1982 Act contains the UK definition of a company's seat. It states:

"A corporation or association has its seat in the United Kingdom if and only if -
(a) it was incorporated or formed under the law of a part of the United Kingdom and has its registered office or some other official address in the United Kingdom; or
(b) its central management and control is exercised in the United Kingdom".

Thus there are two alternative criteria for domicile in the UK. It suffices for one to be established. A company may be domiciled *both* in the UK and abroad.

Once general jurisdiction is established as above, through determining the defendant's domicile, the next step is to apply the rules of special jurisdiction, in order to ascertain whether there is any other State in which he may also be sued. Article 5 provides that:

"A person domiciled in a Contracting State may, in another Contracting State, be sued:
(1) in matters relating to a contract, in the courts for the place of performance of the obligation in question;
(3) in matters relating to tort ...... in the courts for the place where the harmful event occurred;
(5) as regards a dispute arising out of the operations of a branch, agency or other establishment, in the courts for the place in which the branch, agency or other establishment is situated;".

In product liability contract cases under Article 5(1), "the place of performance" will usually be the place of sale or, if different, the place of delivery. Special rules for certain consumer contracts are set out in Articles 13 -14. Subject to the definition in Article 13, Article 14 provides that:

"A consumer may bring proceedings against the other party to a contract either in the courts of the Contracting State in which that party is domiciled or in the courts of the Contracting State in which he is himself domiciled".

If a German company advertises a radio in England to a consumer who is domiciled in England and buys it there, the consumer may sue on the contract in either England or Germany.

Most product liability claims will be governed by Article 5(3). Section 6(7) of the Act provides:

"It is hereby declared that liability by virtue of this Part is to be treated as liability in tort for the purposes of any enactment conferring jurisdiction on any court with respect to any matter".

Thus Article 5(3) applies both to claims under Part I and under the traditional torts such as negligence. A company domiciled in a Convention Territory may, in addition to being sued in that State, also be sued in another Convention Territory "where the harmful event occurred". In *Bier* v *Mines De Potasse* (1976), the European Court considered whether this meant the place where the harmful act was done or the place where injury was suffered. The French defendants operating in Alsace pumped polluting chloride into the river in France which resulted in Bier, a commercial nurseryman near Rotterdam who used the water from the Rhine, incurring expense in purifying it in Holland. The European Court held that Bier could sue in either France or Holland. Thus Article 5(3) grants jurisdiction to the courts of the place where (a) the defendant acted and (b) the plaintiff suffered.

Article 5(5) further extends the scope of jurisdiction by providing that, when a dispute arises out of the operation of a branch or agency, a company domiciled in a Contracting State may also be sued in the Contracting State where the branch or agency is situated. An Italian company with a branch in Belgium may be sued, in disputes arising out of the operation of the branch, in either Italy or Belgium.

Article 6 is a vital provision covering joint defendants, third parties and counterclaims. It states that:

"A person domiciled in a Contracting State may also be sued:

(1) where he is one of a number of defendants, in the courts for the place where any one of them is domiciled;"

Subject to certain conditions, he may also be sued as a third party or on a counterclaim in the court dealing with the original proceedings.

It follows that a company domiciled in a Convention Territory is potentially at risk of being sued in any other Convention territory. This can occur, in certain cases, even though its product is not made in the other State, and even if it is not sold there. A company producing components in England alone may be sued in any other Convention Territory in which the producer of the final product is domiciled or in which the victim suffers damage. Moreover the co-defendant's liability need not arise under Part I of the 1987 Act; Article 6 applies equally where negligence or breach of contract is alleged. Thus the UK producer of a defective drug might find himself sued as co-defendant under Part I of the Act with the allegedly negligent French doctor and pharmacist in France where the drug was prescribed and dispensed, or in Germany where the victim took the drug and was injured.

Article 4 deals with the position of defendants outside the EC:

"If the defendant is not domiciled in a Contracting State, the jurisdiction of the courts of each Contracting State shall, subject to the provisions of Article 16, be determined by the law of that State ......".

Thus the position of a non-EC defendant is governed by the jurisdictional law of the EC State in whose courts the action is brought. Suppose that Nippon CP makes a defective component in Japan, and sells it to an English firm, EI, which supplies it to Pr who proceeds to incorporate it in England into a portable computer which injures V while he is travelling in Denmark. V can sue EI and Pr in England and Denmark. Whether he can join Nippon CP depends on the jurisdiction laws of the State in which he chooses to bring his action.

This is the problem of long-arm jurisdiction. Order 11(1)(f) of the Rules of the Supreme Court states that in such cases:

"service of a writ out of the jurisdiction is permissible with the leave of the Court if in the action begun by the writ ...... the claim is founded on a tort and the damage was sustained, or resulted from an act committed, within the jurisdiction."

As s.6(7) of the 1987 Act provides that liability under Part I is to be treated as liability in tort for jurisdiction purposes, this means that English courts will almost always be entitled to hear product liability claims against defendants domiciled outside the EC. A major criterion in their decision to do so may be whether the foreign producer intended or expected his product to be marketed in the UK. It remains to be seen to what extent English courts will assume such jurisdiction and apply UK law.

2. Other EC States

Any UK producer, own-brander or importer - or even, under s.2(3) of the Act, a supplier who fails to identify them - is in theory potentially liable to be sued in any other Convention Territory. The Directive allows the EC States three options in the ways in which they implement it. Article 15(1) of the Directive states that:

"Each Member State may:
(a) by way of derogation from Article 2, provide in its legislation that within the meaning of Article 1 of this Directive "product" also means primary agricultural products and game;
(b) by way of derogation from Article 7(e), maintain or ...... provide in this legislation that the producer shall be liable even if he proves that the state of scientific

and technical knowledge at the time when he put the product into circulation was not such as to enable the existence of a defect to be discovered."

Article 16 states that:

"Any Member State may provide that a producer's total liability for damage resulting from a death or personal injury and caused by identical items with the same defect shall be limited to an amount which may not be less than 70 million ECU".

Thus there are three main options. First, to include primary agricultural produce and game. Second, to exclude the development risks defence. Third, to impose an overall financial limit of around £45 million on damages payable by a defendant in respect of any one line of defective products.

So far as the authors know, none of the other States has to date taken the view that "product" should include primary agricultural produce and game. If this continues, the law on this point will be uniform throughout the EC.

It is otherwise with the development risks defence. France, Belgium and Luxembourg do not intend to allow it at all. Germany will not include it in cases involving pharmaceutical products in respect of which s.84 of the German Pharmaceuticals Act 1976 imposes strict liability on pharmaceutical manufacturers and producers for death or personal injury suffered by consumers or users of their products. Consequently, three countries will not have the defence, and a fourth will exclude it for pharamaceutical products.

Nor will there be uniformity over whether to set an overall limit of 70 million ECU (about £45 million) on a defendant's total liability for damages resulting from death or personal injuries caused by identical items with the same defect. It is understood that only Germany and one or two other States are in favour of setting such a limit.

These variations increase the premium on forum shopping. Suppose that a UK pharmaceutical firm produces a new drug which turns out to have a defect that seriously injures hundreds of patients but which could not have been discovered in the state of scientific and technical knowledge at the time the firm supplied the drug to its distributors. If the patients are injured by it in England, the development risks defence will apply, so the producers will not be liable. If the patients are injured by it in Germany, the development risks defence will not debar them from recovering damages, but the total of these damages will be limited to 70 million ECU. If the patients are injured by it in France, not only will the development risks defence not debar them but also there will be no limit on the damages they can collectively recover. Those having a choice of where to sue will select the States whose laws will provide the most favourable result.

Such variations between member States are manifestly undesirable in practice. Accordingly Articles 15(3) and 16(2) of the Directive provide that in 1995 the EC Commission will report on their operation to the Council of Ministers which will decide, in particular, whether to repeal the options of the development risks defence and the total financial limit on liability.

3. Claimants

Product liability claimants now have an unprecedented range of remedies. This has arisen in three ways. The result is that they have acquired a wider choice of:

- how to sue, eg in contract or tort or under the Act;
- whom to sue;
- where to sue.

Section 2(6) of the Act states: "This section shall be without prejudice to any liability arising otherwise than by virtue of this Part". Thus the existing laws of contract and tort are expressly preserved, and claims under Part I are added to them. Any combination of the three is possible. If a victim is sold a defective new armchair which collapses and injures

him, his more obvious options are to sue the retailer under
s.14 of the Sale of Goods Act 1979 and/or the producer
under Part I. He can also base his claim in negligence, on
the grounds that the producer ought not to have created the
defect' and/or that the retailer should have discovered it. A
novel but conceivable combination for the retailer would be
claims against him under both s.14(2) of the Sale of Goods
Act 1979 and s.2(3) of the Act, if he is unable to identify the
producer or his last supplier of the defective chair.

Section 2(2) of the Act adds new categories of defendant in
addition to those who are normally sued. In the past, it has
been rare for importers to be sued, and own-branders have
usually only been liable as retailers if at all. Now both can be
sued as if they are producers. Moreover, under s.2(3) of the
Act, suppliers who fail to comply with a request for
identification may be liable under Part I to a victim who did
not even buy the product from them. Consequently, in a
particular case, the injured person may have the choice of
suing any or all of the component part producer, finished
product producer, own-brander and EC importer under the
Act, the designer in negligence and the retailer in contract.
Section 2(5) states that "Where two or more persons are
liable by virtue of this Part for the same damage, their
liability shall be joint and several". This already applies to
product liability cases under the existing laws of contract and
tort. Therefore, if he wishes, the victim may sue only one of
several possible defendants and still recover full damages.
The chosen defendant would be left with his rights under the
Civil Liability (Contribution) Act 1978.

The most spectacular possibilities for product liability victims
lie in the field of forum shopping. There is now a
significantly increased chance of bringing an action
elsewhere in the EC. So far as liability is concerned, there
are two main purposes in this. First, as seen above, the EC
States differ in the ways in which they are exercising their
options under the Directive; claimants confronted with a
development risks defence or a total financial limit will seek
to sue in a State that does not allow it. Second, the EC
States' existing laws of contract and tort remain in force;

these are still unharmonised so, in a case in which Part I does not apply, for instance because the defect arose after the product was supplied, it is vital for claimants to select the State whose laws are the most favourable.

The example on page 97 suggested that the English producer of a defective drug, apart from being sued in the UK, might find himself sued as co-defendant under Part I of the Act with the allegedly negligent French doctor and pharmacist in France where the drug was prescribed, or in Germany where the victim took the drug and was injured. Suppose that the defect in the drug could not have been discovered in the state of scientific and technical knowledge at the time of its supply. The injured person has the option of suing the English producer and/or the French doctor and pharmacist. The proceedings may be brought in England, France or Germany. England is apt to be avoided, as it permits the development risks defence. If the drug injures numerous other people, it might be unwise to sue in Germany since it imposes a limit on the total liability for damages. Before finally deciding to proceed in France, the injured person should consider the practical matters set out below.

This is because claimants' choice of venue will not only be determined by variations in substantive law. It may also be affected by the following practical and procedural factors in the eligible countries (the list is closely based on a similar list prepared by Simon Pearl, Solicitor, who presented it at the Drug Law Symposium):

(a) the level of legal costs;
(b) who pays them if the case is won or lost;
(c) the availability of legal aid;
(d) the level of damages;
(e) the existence of a jury system;
(f) the quality of the judiciary;
(g) the likely delay before a hearing;
(h) the extent to which an appeal is possible;
(i) the quality of local lawyers;
(j) the inconvenience to opponents;
(k) the rules of disclosure of documents;

(l) the rules on interrogatories and evidence on oath;
(m) the availability of media pressure;
(n) access to and availability of appropriate experts;
(o) access to and availability of factual witnesses;
(p) previous results in product liability cases;
(q) the existence of individuals with similar claims to enable:
- the pooling of resources in one jurisdiction;
- the diversification of proceedings in many jurisdictions.

Thus a claimant in an international product liability case may have a considerable choice how, whom and where to sue. The decision will be based on differences in the law, procedure and practice between the various States in which court action can be taken.

4. The control of risk

Confronted as they are by the improved position of claimants, producers and other potential defendants to product liability claims must take measures to protect themselves:

- they must reduce the risks of their being sued;
- they must transfer as many as possible of the reduced risks;
- they must insure or otherwise budget for the risks that remain.

The need for an organised policy along these lines is shared to a greater or lesser extent by manufacturers, distributors, retailers, own-branders and EC importers. Manufacturers must consider all aspects. Distributors and retailers, who are only liable under Part I in limited circumstances, may be more selective. Special problems encountered by own-branders and EC importers are considered at the end. Accordingly the outline of this section is as follows:

(a) Risk reduction
- quality control

- advertising and promotion
- instructions and warnings
- recalls

(b) Risk transfer
- record retention
- disclosure of documents
- contract terms

(c) Risk retention
- insurance
- budgeting

(d) Special cases
- own-branders
- EC importers
- sale of company

(a) Risk reduction

Quality control: In reducing risks, quality control plays an important part. This is not simply a matter of inspecting and testing the finished product. If the defect is in a component, the producer of the final product is liable as well as the component producer. Accordingly, a manufacturer who buys parts and assembles them into a product must satisfy himself as to the quality of those parts. He should ask his suppliers to carry out suitable tests on the parts and components that they supply and, as far as possible, he should further check their quality. It is prudent to purchase components only from well reputed, easily identifiable and manifestly solvent component producers. Well reputed, so it is less likely that the parts made by them contain a defect. Easily identifiable, so they can be joined in court proceedings and ordered to pay all or some of the damages. Manifestly solvent, so they will be able to satisfy any judgment against them. Solvency in this context includes insurance; the manufacturer of a final product should check that his component producers are suitably insured against product liability claims.

Advertising and promotion: Another aspect of risk reduction is implicit in s.3 of the Act. This defines "defect" so that a product is defective if its safety is not such as persons generally are entitled to expect. In determining this, there is to be taken into account the marketing and advertising of the product, its presentation, and instructions and warnings supplied with it. The temptation in marketing and advertising is to stress a product's safety. It is important to avoid exaggeration, however, because unjustifiable claims may lead to a defect being deemed to exist. Persons generally might associate certain risks with hair dyes, but if the producer of a hair dye advertises it as perfectly safe for everyone, his product will be held defective if it causes injury. In addition to avoiding undue boasts over safety, producers should also state if there are any significant hazards. At this stage, honesty is the best policy in avoiding product liability claims.

Instructions and warnings: Appropriate instructions and warnings are important. They must be clear, comprehensible and appropriate to all kinds of purchaser. It is desirable to distinguish between what is harmful to the product and harmful to the user; in the latter case headings such as "danger" or "warning" are needed. Instructions and warnings can be contained in a manual or attached to the product. If the latter, they must be securely attached, since an item may be deemed safe if a suitable warning label is attached but defective if it is removed. If instructions and warnings accompany foreign goods, they must be accurately translated. It will not suffice for an EC importer to supply goods with the instructions or warnings in Japanese.

Recalls: If a product nevertheless proves to be defective, the risk of claims can be reduced by an effective product recall policy. Accordingly it assists to create, if possible, a system to enable products to be traced after supply. A producer is less likely to be found negligent, if he orders a recall as soon as a widespread defect becomes apparent. Whilst a recall will not affect his liability under Part I, since this is not dependent on his innocence or fault, it will nevertheless reduce the level of injuries and therefore the number of claims. A further feature of a recall is that an owner who fails to comply with it may be found guilty of contributory negligence if he is subsequently injured by the product.

(b) Risk transfer

Record retention: Risks that cannot be eliminated must be transferred where possible. A vital aspect of this is adequate record keeping. A producer of finished products should keep, in particular, records of:

    (i)   research and trials on any new type of product, since these are relevant to any development risks defence;

    (ii) the identity of the producers of the components and raw materials, since they will also be liable under Part I for any defect in their product;

    (iii) the dates on which those producers supplied the components and raw materials;

    (iv) the dates on which he (the final producer) supplied the final product.

The time of supply is crucial throughout Part I since:

    (i)   producers are not liable for defects in a product arising after their supply of it: s.4(1)(d);

    (ii) the development risks defence is assessed according to the state of scientific and technical knowledge at the time of this supply: s.4(1)(e);

    (iii) producers are not liable under Part I for any product supplied before it came into force: s.50(7);

    (iv) the ten year longstop limitation period runs from the date of their supply of the product.

Own-branders and EC importers need to keep records of the identity of the manufacturer, the date on which he supplied the product to them, and the date on which they supplied the product to another. Suppliers and other intermediaries liable to be sued must keep:

    (i)   any details they may have of the identity of the producer, own-brander or EC importer;

    (ii) records of the exact identity (and preferably also the business address) of their own supplier;

    (iii) notes of the date and substance of any request made to them to identify one or more of the producer, own-brander or EC importer.

Ideally records should be retained for ten years from the date of the producer's supply: the longstop limitation period. Where this ideal is unattainable in practice, a period of five years is reasonable. To ease storage problems, the records may be transferred onto microfilm. This will be acceptable in any legal proceedings.

Disclosure of documents: Relevant records and documents may have to be disclosed to a claimant. Section 33 of the Supreme Court Act 1981 empowers a court to order discovery where appropriate, even if court action has not been commenced, against anyone who is likely to be a party to the proceedings. Section 34 provides that, once court action is started, a similar order can be made even against a company that is not a party to the proceedings. Thus a component producer, for example, might be ordered to disclose documents in a court action against the producer of the finished product. Order 24 Rule 2 of the Supreme Court Rules provides that, after close of pleadings, the parties to the proceedings must exchange lists of all documents in their possession, custody or power that are relevant to the issues in dispute. How extensive such discovery can be is illustrated by the case of *Board* v *Thomas Hedley & Co Ltd* (1951), a dermatitis case in which the producers of Tide washing powder, who had already disclosed all complaints and congratulatory letters received by them about the product before the plaintiff purchased and used it, were ordered also to disclose all complaints received from subsequent users. The main limitation on discovery is that a party is not required to disclose privileged documents, eg correspondence with its legal advisers about the claim, or a report on the product prepared for the purpose of the litigation.

The company staff concerned need to keep in mind the wide range of documents that may fall to be disclosed in court proceedings and to act accordingly. An apologetic letter from a Customer Relations Officer, thanking the consumer for "pointing out the defect" might prove to be damning evidence later. Defendants must also disclose the originals of relevant letters received, including comments that they have written on them. Consequently, if company staff write on letters of claim or complaint remarks like "Oh dear, not another one" or "This is a real mess-up", they are apt to find their words preserved for legal posterity. Another sensitive area involves internal reports on accidents or complaints. Such a report is privileged from production only if its dominant purpose was for submission to a legal adviser for advice and use in litigation: *Waugh* v *British Railways Board* (1979). If a report is prepared for significant other purposes as well, eg establishing the cause of the accident so that suitable safety measures can be taken, it must be disclosed to the claimant's solicitors in court action.

Contract terms: The other main method of transferring risks is through suitable contract terms. Many products give rise to a chain of contracts between:

- manufacturer and distributor;
- distributor and retailer;
- retailer and purchaser.

Therefore the position of manufacturers, retailers and distributors will be considered in turn.

Manufacturers of finished products may seek to insert into their conditions of purchase clauses covering the quality of components and raw materials bought by them or warranties that such goods are not defective or that they have been tested and conform to all relevant standards. They may also wish to negotiate an indemnity from the supplier of their raw materials or components against claims arising out of defects in them. In addition, a manufacturer may include in his standard conditions of sale an exclusion or limitation of liability clause, restricting his liability to his distributors in the event of a consumer claiming against one of them, coupled with an indemnity from his distributors in the event of the claim being made against the manufacturer.

Retailers will wish to pass liability back to the producer, or at least far enough back along the chain of supply to escape liability themselves. Their conditions of purchase should therefore include warranties from the producer/distributor that the product conforms to all accepted safety standards and has been tested either as thoroughly as possible or in accordance with legal requirements. They should also consider where possible taking indemnities from the producer or wholesaler against claims and loss arising from a defective product.

Distributors caught in the middle of the chain of supply should build appropriate conditions into both their conditions of purchase and of sale, together with a stipulation that their conditions prevail over those of the parties with whom they deal. This will arm them better for any dispute in the "battle of forms". In reality, larger companies tend to impose their conditions on smaller ones. Accordingly, small intermediary companies need to study with special care the wording of contracts into which they enter.

Contract terms and conditions, of course, normally depend on securing the agreement of the other party to the contract. Moreover they are subject to the Unfair Contract Terms Act 1977.

(c) Risk retention

Insurance: Risks that cannot be reduced or transferred are of necessity retained. They must then be either insured or funded within the company. It is important that any insurance policy takes account of both major recent changes in the law. First, the strict liability imposed on a wider range of possible defendants by Part I of the Consumer Protection Act 1987. Second, the increased chance of being sued in a foreign State as a result of the Civil Jurisdiction and Judgments Act 1982. It is also necessary to keep in mind that defences available in the UK (eg development risks) may not be permitted elsewhere and that certain other countries have far higher levels of damages.

Budgeting: In so far as a company cannot, or chooses not

to, insure its product liability risks, it must consider financial planning to meet them. The most obvious expedient is to create a reserve fund by putting aside a certain amount each year.

(d) Special cases

Own-branders: Section 2(2)(b) imposes strict liability on any person who, by putting his name on the product or using a trade or other distinguishing mark in relation to the product, has held himself out to be the producer of the product. Thus supermarkets and chainstores, for instance, may attract liability in respect of own-brand goods, although they did not produce them. Consequently the fundamental question for an own-brander is whether to continue to be one. There are two alternative ways of ceasing this if desired. First, he can remove his name, trade mark or other distinguishing feature. Second, he can make it clear that he is not the producer of the product. Those who continue to be own-branders should check and if necessary negotiate an addition to their insurance policies.

EC importers: Importers from outside the EC are vulnerable through the combination of being treated as a producer under s.2 of the Act and obtaining their products from often distant countries. They are strictly liable under s.2. Yet their rights to contribution or indemnity may often be difficult to enforce. Importers from the Far East, for instance, need to be specially careful to check the reputation, identity and solvency of the producers whose goods they import. They must ensure that instructions, warnings and statements about the product's intended use are accurately translated. And their product liability insurance policies may require review, in order to be certain that they cover the importers' new liability for goods that they have not produced.

Sale of company: If a company is sold, its product liability position must be considered. Where it is sold whole, its value will be discounted so as to reflect its accrued and future uninsured liability for defective products. Either the price paid will simply be less, or the vendor of the company will have to enter into an indemnity against any uninsured product liability claim. An alternative to selling the whole company is to dispose of it as a collection of assets at its full value, leaving behind the legal identity of the company with its accrued liabilities. This is legitimate, unless it is proved that the assets of a company are being deliberately transferred in order to avoid product liability or other claims.

5. Limited liability companies

This leads to a difficult area of the law. The problems are indicated by the following exchange in the House of Lords during the Committee stage of the Bill:

> "*Lord Williams of Elvel:* Before we leave Clause 1, perhaps I may raise one matter for clarification on the interpretation of the expression 'producer'? May I put my question in the form of an example? Suppose ABC Company either develops a new product or has a product which already exists. It manufactures that product and it markets it. Suppose, furthermore, that ABC Company vests in a subsidiary its patent, its trademark and its manufacturing facility of either the new product or the existing product. Suppose the subsidiary is capitalised at £100 and suppose the rest of the financing for the subsidiary, the manufacturing and all the rest of it are guaranteed by the parent company but are obviously not in the capital base of the subsidiary.

> In the circumstances - and this is the simple case; I have not got to the foreign cases and licence cases - who is the producer? Is it the subsidiary? ......

> If that product causes damage, against whom can the person who is damaged have recourse under the product liability provisions of the Bill? It would seem to me to be against the subsidiary. If that is the case, and if the subsidiary is only capitalised at £100 and if, say, the damages were assessed at £1 million, then the parent company can simply put its subsidiary into bankruptcy and the doctrine of limited liability does not give the

parent company any responsibility at all for the subsequent debts of the bankrupt subsidiary. Am I right or am I wrong?

Lord Lucas of Chilworth: I believe that the noble Lord is right ......

Lord Williams of Elvel: I am grateful to the noble Lord. Does not this render the whole of Part I, the product liability, relatively nugatory, because any company can, and indeed will in practice, put their operations for different products into subsidiaries, particularly developing new products? That is a question to which the Government have to respond seriously. If companies can isolate themselves by this financial mechanism, if you like, it renders the Bill ineffective.

Lord Lucas of Chilworth: I do not believe for one moment that the situation is likely to arise, because I think it would be too difficult practically to do that. However, the noble Lord will of course appreciate it when I say that I shall look carefully at what he has said.

In looking at it, as I shall, I hope that the noble Lord opposite will also think of these points. Perhaps the liability that we foresee - or perhaps it is more true to say the liability that we do not foresee; but suppose there was a liability arising under Part I - would be only very occasionally large enough to justify, certainly in commercial terms, the sacrifice of a subsidiary. Even then I suggest, the question would arise only if the liability implicit in what the noble Lord has said has not been adequately insured.

If a group of companies is large enough to be able to sacrifice a subsidiary, surely it is much more likely that it would be able to either bear the financial loss or to have secured adequate insurance in the first place. I do not think that it would want to sacrifice a subsidiary in the kind of scenario that the noble Lord painted, with the consequences for the reputation of the whole group. We should also remember that there are other statutes which would inhibit it so doing. The noble Lord himself will clearly remember, as I remember, the provisions of the Insolvency Act, which impose duties on the directors. They are not ones that they can easily walk away from purely by taking the course of action that the noble Lod poses that they might take ......

Lord Williams of Elvel: I am grateful to the noble Lord. What we are now down to is whether a parent company considers its reputation sufficiently important to it not to abandon its subsidiary, or whether the directors of that subsidiary happen to be people who are covered under the Insolvency Act. I can invent all sorts of scenarios for the noble Lord, and I am sure any noble Lord can do so. We can put it in a trust company; we can vest it in a trust company in Gibraltar, or in the Cayman Islands; we can do all sorts of things, and people do this.

The point of the Bill, as I understand it, is to make it a strict product legal liability. If we are down to the question of whether a parent company would sacrifice its subsidiary we are down to the question of whether a parent company believes its reputation would be harmed, and that is a quite different issue from the question of making it legally liable.

Lord Lucas of Chilworth: I find it very difficult to believe - because perhaps I am a naive man - that companies will engage in a number of those practices which the noble Lord opposite thinks may happen. I dare say that a number of noble Lords could paint a variety of scenarios, all to the detriment of some producer who wants to escape his moral as well as his legal responsibilities. I do not believe that business is conducted in that way. I believe that the provisions of the Bill are sufficient to persuade him to a proper course of action ...."

This debate illustrates a general rule. An injured claimant, although he succeeds in establishing liability, will not always be able to recover his damages. As suggested above, liability may be vested in a subsidiary or licensee company which lacks the means to satisfy the claim. Alternatively, the producer or other defendant may become bankrupt or the defendant company may already in good faith have sold its assets to a successor company (which is not itself liable, because it is not the producer or other defendant within s.2 of the Act), with the result that the defendant company cannot meet any fresh legal liabilities that arise. At least the above difficulties are all readily capable of resolution, provided that the liable company still exists as a legal entity and has appropriate insurance covering the product liability.

More intractable problems arise if a company is dissolved and/or was uninsured. An uninsured company that is dissolved is not worth suing, even when this can be achieved technically, because any assets will have been distributed. Moreover it is impossible, once a company has been dissolved for more than two years following a voluntary liquidation, for the dissolution to be declared void so that it can be sued. Suppose that P Ltd produces and supplies a defective product in 1988, is dissolved in 1989 after a voluntary liquidation and that Mr V is injured by the product in 1992. Mr V cannot sue P Ltd so, even if P Ltd was insured, he cannot obtain a judgment to enforce against the insurers.

These are matters of general company law. They affect product liability law, however, in that however strict the legal liability for defective products is made, this cannot afford greater protection to injured persons than company law permits. Strict liability in law does not mean inevitable compensation in practice.

Chapter 6

Consumer safety legislation

Part II of the Act deals with consumer safety legislation. When it comes into force it will repeal and replace the existing consumer safety legislation, which is contained in the Consumer Safety Act 1978 and the Consumer Safety (Amendment) Act 1986. At the time of writing (June 1987), it is uncertain when Part II will come into force and, accordingly, it is necessary to be aware of both existing legislation and Part II of the Act; the former to appreciate the present law and the latter to plan for forthcoming changes.

1. Existing legislation

The Consumer Protection Act 1961

The starting point for the present legislation was the Consumer Protection Act 1961. It contained provisions which:

(a) empowered the Secretary of State to introduce regulations imposing safety requirements on types of goods if he considered it necessary to avoid or lessen any risk of death or personal injury (s.1); and

(b) prohibited the sale of goods which were in breach of regulations imposed under s.1 (s.2); and

(c) allowed anyone adversely affected by a breach of s.2 to make a claim in civil law against the person in breach on the ground of breach of statutory duty (s.3); and

(d) made it a criminal offence to be in breach of s.2 (s.3(2)).

Various regulations were introduced under the 1961 Act, examples of which are:

(a) the Stands for Carry-cots (Safety) Regulations 1966 which, *inter alia,* require a guard rail or stops to keep carry-cots in position;

(b) the Toys (Safety) Regulations 1974 which contain various rules concerning the composition and construction of toys and the use of plastic bags for packing;

(c) the Oil Heaters (Safety) Regulations 1977 which impose safety requirements for oil heaters - for example oil heaters must have a self-extinguishing facility.

The Consumer Safety Act 1978

During the 1970s there was concern that the measures contained in the 1961 Act were too limited. This concern was reflected in a Green Paper on Consumer Safety published by the Government in February 1976, the result of which was the Consumer Safety Act 1978. It was designed to strengthen legislative control of goods available to the public. Since it was intended that the 1978 Act would replace the 1961 Act, it contained provisions which not only were innovatory but also those which were similar to those in the 1961 Act. Before dealing with these, the 1978 Act definition of "goods" must be considered. By virtue of s.9(4) "goods" include:

"substances whether natural or manufactured and whether or not incorporated in or mixed with other goods".

Goods do not, however, include:

(a) "food as defined in the Food Act 1984", which definition is - "food includes drink, chewing gum and other products of a like nature and use, and articles and substances used as ingredients in the preparation of food or drink or of such products but does not include water, live animals or birds, fodder or feeding stuffs for animals, birds or fish, or articles or substances used only as drugs"; or

(b) "feeding stuff and fertiliser"; or

(c) "medicinal products".

The 1978 Act, therefore, covers goods such as lawnmowers, electric blankets, electric fires, hairdryers, ovens, washing machines, but not items such as hamburgers, manure or cough medicine.

The 1978 Act contains the following provisions similar to those in the 1961 Act:

(a) By s.1 the Secretary of State may make such regulations as he considers appropriate to ensure that goods are safe or to ensure that appropriate information about the goods is provided with them. The regulations may relate to the composition or contents, design, construction, finish or packing of goods. For example, The Toy Water Snakes (Safety) Order 1983 prohibits the supply of any toy water snake filled with water containing specified bacteria or organisms.

The regulations may also require conformity with a certain standard, or the testing of goods in a certain manner for compliance with the regulations or the display of a warning relating to the goods. For example, the Upholstered Furniture (Safety) Regulations 1980 require, *inter alia,* the display of warning notices to the effect that "careless use of cigarettes and matches could set fire to this furniture".

(b) Section 2 makes it a criminal offence for any person to supply goods in a form contrary to that required by safety regulations. The penalty for such an offence is a fine not exceedng £2000 and/or 3 months imprisonment.

(c) Section 6 stipulates that "any obligation imposed on a person by safety regulations or a prohibition order or a prohibition notice is a duty owed by him to any other person who may be affected by a failure to perform the obligation, and a breach of that duty is actionable (subject to the defences and other incidents applying to actions for breach of statutory duty)". This establishes the right to make a claim in civil law for damages for breach of statutory duty.

The 1978 Act introduced new provisions, not previously contained in the 1961 Act, as follows:

(a) Section 3 introduced the concept of "prohibition orders", "prohibition notices" and "notices to warn". A prohibition order is an order by the Secretary of State prohibiting the supply of goods which are considered unsafe. For example, the Scented Erasers (Safety) Order 1984 prohibited a person from supplying any eraser smelling of food or flowers which has any two dimensions which are less than 45 millimetres. (This order expired on 30 January 1984 and its provisions were replaced by those in the Food Imitations (Safety) Regulations 1985).

A prohibition notice is the notice which the Secretary of State is empowered to serve on any person prohibiting the supply of goods considered to be unsafe and specified in the notice.

A notice to warn is a notice which the Secretary of State is empowered to serve on any person requiring the person "to publish, in a form and manner and on occasions specified in the notice and at his own expense, a warning about any goods so supplied which the Secretary of State considers are not safe and which the person supplies or has supplied."

(b) The 1961 Act stipulated that no person should "sell or have in his possession for the purpose of selling" goods which contravened safety regulations and in certain circumstances applied to hire or hire-purchase transactions. The 1978 Act extends the circumstances in which there will be breach of safety regulations to "supplying or offering or agreeing to supply goods or exposing or possessing goods for supply". This is a material extension. For example, the 1961 Act did not cover situations when goods were offered as prizes whereas the 1978 Act does.

(c) By section 4, the Secretary of State has the right to obtain information about any goods whose safety he considers to be uncertain from any person who may be in a position to provide relevant information. Solicitors and barristers, however, are exempted from disclosing any information given to them in a privileged communication.

(d) Section 5 imposes upon weights and measures authorities a duty to enforce the provisions of the Act within the area for which they are responsible. Under the 1961 Act, weights and measures authorities had a discretion, not a duty, to enforce that Act.

(e) The 1961 Act gave powers to the Secretary of State in respect of goods if it was thought necessary to take action to "prevent or reduce risk of death or personal injury". The 1978 Act extended the circumstances in which the Secretary of State could act by having as its primary criterion whether goods can be considered "safe". Section 9 of the 1978 Act defined safe as meaning "such as to prevent or adequately to reduce any risk of death and any risk of personal injury from the goods in question or from circumstances in which the goods might be used or kept".

As has already been mentioned, it was intended that the 1978 Act would replace the 1961 Act. However, safety regulations introduced by virtue of the 1961 Act derived their authority from that Act and until safety regulations have been made under the 1978 Act to replace those safety regulations, the 1961 Act will stay in force for the sole purpose of giving effect to regulations introduced under it.

The Consumer Safety (Amendment) Act 1986

Although the 1978 Act strengthened the Secretary of State's powers to seek to remove from the UK market goods which created the risk of injury or death, there was concern that its provisions were still too limited. This concern arose particularly over difficulties of enforcement in respect of unsafe imported goods. Accordingly the Department of Trade reviewed the 1978 Act and this resulted in a

Government White Paper entitled *The Safety of Goods* (Cmnd 9302, 1984). In that White Paper the basic proposal was to:

"introduce a general duty on all suppliers to ensure that the goods they supply are safe in accordance with sound modern standards of safety ..... Sound modern standards of safety would be defined in terms of the standard of reasonable safety a person is entitled to expect, bearing in mind considerations such as cost, and the extent to which safe, proven and recognised technology is available".

This government White Paper resulted in the Consumer Safety (Amendment) Act 1986 and also in the new consumer safety legislation contained in Part II of the Act, which is considered later in this chapter.

The 1986 Act introduced, *inter alia,* the following provisions:

(a) By ss.1 and 2 the Commissioners of Customs and Excise are entitled to disclose information relating to imported goods to weights and measures authorities and, if the authorities consider it appropriate, to seize and detain goods for up to 48 hours.

(b) Section 3 entitles weights and measures authorities to serve "suspension notices" on any person thought to be involved in the supply of goods which are in breach of the 1978 Act or any safety regulations. A suspension notice prohibits the supply of such goods for up to six months. Appeals against the detention of goods or the effect of suspension notices can be made to the magistrates' court or any other court in which a prosecution has been commenced.

(c) Section 4 introduces a defence to prosecutions for breach of safety regulations. By virtue of s.4(2) "it shall be a defence for that person (ie a person against whom proceedings for breach of safety regulations have been taken) to show that he took all reasonable steps and exercised all due diligence to avoid committing the offence".

This is a very important provision. It makes it clear

that there is not strict liability under existing consumer safety legislation. Provided a defendant can prove that all reasonable and proper steps have been taken, conviction will be avoided. This defence may well involve the allegation that there was an act of default on the part of another person or reliance on information supplied by another. In the former case, any defendant making such an allegation must, more than seven days before the hearing, advise the prosecution of this.

If the defence involves reliance on information supplied by another, s.4(5) will apply. It states that "a person shall not be entitled to rely on the defence ...... by reason of his reliance on information supplied by another, unless he shows that it was reasonable in all the circumstances for him to have relied on the information, having regard in particular -

(a) to the steps which he took, and those which might reasonably have been taken, for the purpose of verifying the information; and

(b) to whether he had any reason to disbelieve the information."

2. Part II of the 1987 Act

When Part II comes into force - and, at June 1987, no date has been set - it will replace the existing legislation described above. What follows is an outline of its principal provisions by reference to the circumstances in which liability will arise, defences to prosecutions and enforcement.

Liability

Section 10 makes it a criminal offence to supply, offer or agree to supply or expose or possess for supply "consumer goods" which fail to comply with "the general safety requirement". By "the general safety requirement" is meant whether or not the goods are reasonably safe having regard to all the circumstances, including:

(a) the manner in which, and purposes for which, the goods are being or would be marketed, the get-up of the goods, the use of any mark in relation to the goods and any instructions or warnings regarding their keeping, use or consumption; and

(b) any standards of safety relating to the goods in question (ie is there a failure to comply with any published standards of safety contained in, for example, voluntary standards adopted by trade associations); and

(c) the existence of any means by which it would have been reasonable (taking into account the cost, likelihood and extent of any improvement) for the goods to have been made safer.

Part II also defines, in s.19, what it means by safe, namely:

"that there is no risk, or no risk apart from one reduced to a minimum, that any of the following will ...... cause the death of, or any personal injury to, any person whatsoever, that is to say -

(a) the goods;

(b) the keeping, use or consumption of the goods;

(c) the assembly of any of the goods which are, or are to be, supplied unassembled;

(d) any emission or leakage from the goods or, as a result of the keeping, use or consumption of the goods, from anything else; or

(e) reliance on the accuracy of any measurement, calculation or other reading made by or by means of the goods."

Consumer goods are defined in s.10(7) as:

"any goods which are ordinarily intended for private use or consumption, not being -

(a) growing crops or things comprised in land by virtue of being attached to it;

(b) water, food, feeding stuff or fertiliser;

(c) gas;

(d) aircraft (other than hang-gliders) or motor vehicles;

(e) controlled drugs or licensed medicinal products;

(f) tobacco."

Section 10 will introduce a new concept of liability to consumer safety legislation. The existing legislation will only give rise to an offence if the Secretary of State is aware of goods which are unsafe, introduces regulations relating to those goods and a supplier is in breach of those regulations. Section 10 introduces a general duty to ensure that goods are safe, breach of which will be an offence. It will provide greater protection for consumers but will impose greater duties on suppliers. No longer will it be sufficient merely to be aware of safety regulations. It will be necessary for all suppliers of consumer goods to be aware of the properties, composition and likely uses of the goods which they supply and to consider whether or not they are safe; if they create a risk of injury or death, an offence under s.10 will be committed.

Section 11 contains provisions whereby the Secretary of State can introduce safety regulations. These are similar to those in the 1978 Act and will therefore not be considered further save to mention that it is s.12 which makes it a criminal offence to be in breach of safety regulations.

Section 13 provides the Secretary of State with the authority to serve prohibition notices or notices to warn and s.18 contains the Secretary of State's power to obtain information about goods. Section 14 deals with suspension notices. Again these provisions are similar to those in the 1978 Act. Section 13(4) makes it an offence to contravene prohibition notices or notices to warn, s.14(6) to breach a suspension notice, and s.18(3) to fail to comply with a request for information.

Defences

There are five defences which may be available to a prosecution for breach of s.10. These are as follows:
   (a) the defendant can show that failure to comply with the general safety requirement resulted from compliance with "any requirement imposed by or under any enactment or with any Community obligation" (s.10(3)(a)); or the defendant can show that there has

been full compliance with any safety regulations or safety standards imposed under safety regulations (s.10(3)(b)); or

(b) the defendant "reasonably believed that the goods would not be used or consumed in the United Kingdom" (s.10(4)(a)); or

(c) the defendant supplied the goods in the course of a retail business and at the time of supply neither knew nor had reasonable grounds for believing that the goods failed to comply with the general safety requirement (s.10(4)(b)). This is important for retailers and at least affords them the opportunity of a possible defence, rather than facing strict liability in circumstances where they would have no reason whatever to suppose goods to be unsafe; or

(d) the terms of supply "indicated that the goods were not supplied or to be supplied as new goods" and "provided for, or contemplated, the acquisition of an interest in the goods by the persons supplied or to be supplied" (s.10(4)(c)); or

(e) the defendant took all reasonable steps and exercised all due diligence to avoid committing the offence (s.39(1)). As in s.12 of the Consumer Safety (Amendment) Act 1986 there are provisions relating to allegations of fault by another or reliance on information supplied by another in s.39(2) and (4) and these provisions mirror those in s.12 of the 1986 Act.

Part II of the Act will not impose strict liability. There are defences to allegations of breach of s.10, and the s.39 defence is stated to apply to alleged failure to comply with statutory regulations or prohibition notices or notices to warn or suspension notices. There will, however, be no defence to an allegation of failure to comply with a request for information under s.18, unless the Secretary of State fails to follow the correct procedure or the defendant can show "reasonable cause" for his failure to comply.

Enforcement

Section 27 of the Act makes it "the duty of every weights and measures authority in Great Britain to enforce within their area the safety provisions" of the Act. Sections 28 and 34 contain various powers to assist weights and measures authorities in their enforcement of Part II of the Act:

(a) Section 28 provides authority for test purchases of consumer goods but also establishes that any person who is a party to subsequent proceedings can himself have the goods tested. It is important for any potential defendant to be aware of this facility and to take advantage of it, particularly if there is doubt about the results of the weights and measures authority's test.

(b) Section 29 authorises officers of the relevant weights and measures authority, for the purpose of ascertaining whether there has been a breach of any safety provisions, to -
- inspect any goods and enter any premises other than those occupied solely as a private residence;
- examine any procedure connected with the production of any goods;
- require the production of records and/or seize goods if the goods are believed to have been imported into the UK;
- seize and detain records relating to the business.

These are wide reaching powers. It is important for all suppliers to be aware of them and the authors recommend that, particularly where there is the possibility of seizure of records, any supplier so affected seeks immediate legal advice and advises the enforcement officer that this is being sought, with the request that his inspection await the arrival of the supplier's legal representatives.

(c) Section 30 allows the grant of search warrants where it is believed by enforcement officers that entry or access may be refused.

(d) Section 31 allows customs officers to detain goods for not more than two working days, and working days exclude Saturdays, Sundays or Bank Holidays.

(e) Section 32 makes it an offence to obstruct or to give false information to an enforcement officer.

(f) Section 33 sets out the manner in which an appeal can

be made against the seizure of goods and s.34 the circumstances in which the weights and measures authority will have to pay compensation for the wrongful seizure of goods.

There is one final point to note about Part II of the Act. Section 41 provides:

"An obligation imposed by safety regulations shall be a duty owed to any person who may be affected by a contravention of the obligation and, subject to any provision to the contrary in the regulations and to the defences and other incidents applying to actions for breach of statutory duty, a contravention of any such obligation shall be actionable accordingly".

Thus, breach of the safety regulations will enable a claim for damages for breach of statutory duty to be brought.

Appendix 1

The European Communities Directive

The Council of the European Communities Directive of 25 July 1985 on the approximation of the laws, regulations and administrative provisions of the Member States concerning liability for defective products

The Council of the European Communities,
Having regard to the Treaty establishing the European Economic Community, and in particular Article 100 thereof,
Having regard to the proposal from the Commission,
Having regard to the opinion of the European Parliament,
Having regard to the opinion of the Economic and Social Committee,

Whereas approximation of the laws of the Member States concerning the liability of the producer for damage caused by the defectiveness of his products is necessary because the existing divergences may distort competition and affect the movement of goods within the common market and entail a differing degree of protection of the consumer against damage caused by a defective product to his health or property;

Whereas liability without fault on the part of the producer is the sole means of adequately solving the problem, peculiar to our age of increasing technicality, of a fair apportionment of the risks inherent in modern technological production;

Whereas liability without fault should apply only to movables which have been industrially produced; whereas, as a result, it is appropriate to exclude liability for agricultural products and game, except where they have undergone a processing of an industrial nature which could cause a defect in these products; whereas the liability provided for in this Directive should also apply to movables which are used in the construction of immovables or are installed in immovables;

Whereas protection of the consumer requires that all producers involved in the production process should be made liable, in so far as their finished product, component part or any raw material supplied by them was defective; whereas, for the same reason, liability should extend to importers of products into the Community and to persons who present themselves as producers by affixing their name, trade mark or other distinguishing feature or who supply a product the producer of which cannot be identified;

Whereas, in situations where several persons are liable for the same damage, the protection of the consumer requires that the injured person should be able to claim full compensation for the damage from any one of them;

Whereas, to protect the physical well-being and property of the consumer, the defectiveness of the product should be determined by reference not to its fitness for use but to the lack of the safety which the public at large is entitled to expect; whereas the safety is assessed by excluding any misuse of the product not reasonable under the circumstances;

Whereas a fair apportionment of risk between the injured person and the producer implies that the producer should be able to free himself from liability if he furnishes proof as to the existence of certain exonerating circumstances;

Whereas the protection of the consumer requires that the liability of the producer remains unaffected by acts or omissions of other persons having contributed to cause the damage; whereas, however, the contributory negligence of the injured person may be taken into account to reduce or disallow such liability;

Whereas the protection of the consumer requires compensation for death and personal injury as well as compensation for damage to property; whereas the latter should nevertheless be limited to goods for private use or consumption and be subject to a deduction of a lower threshold of a fixed amount in order to avoid litigation in an excessive number of cases; whereas this Directive should not prejudice compensation for pain and suffering and other non-material damages payable, where appropriate, under the law applicable to the case;

Whereas a uniform period of limitation for the bringing of action for compensation is in the interests both of the injured person and of the producer;

Whereas products age in the course of time, higher safety standards are developed and the state of science and technology progresses; whereas, therefore, it would not be reasonable to make the producer liable for an unlimited period for the defectiveness of his product; whereas, therefore, liability should expire after a reasonable length of time, without prejudice to claims pending at law;

Whereas, to achieve effective protection of consumers, no contractual derogation should be permitted as regards the liability of the producer in relation to the injured person;

Whereas under the legal systems of the Member States an injured party may have a claim for damages based on grounds of contractual liability or on grounds of non-contractual liability other than that provided for in this Directive; in so far as these provisions also serve to attain the objective of effective protection of consumers, they should remain unaffected by this Directive; whereas, in so far as effective protection of consumers in the sector of pharmaceutical products is already also attained in a Member State under a special liability system, claims based on this system should similarly remain possible;

Whereas, to the extent that liability for nuclear injury or damage is already covered in all Member States by adequate special rules, it has been possible to exclude damage of this type from the scope of this Directive;

Whereas, since the exclusion of primary agricultural products and game from the scope of this Directive may be felt, in certain Member States, in view of what is expected for the protection of consumers, to restrict unduly such protection, it should be possible for a Member State to extend liability to such products;

Whereas, for similar reasons, the possibility offered to a producer to free himself from liability if he proves that the state of scientific and technical knowledge at the time when he put the product into circulation was not such as to enable the existence of a defect to be discovered may be felt in certain Member States to restrict unduly the protection of the consumer; whereas it should therefore be possible for a Member State to maintain in its legislation or to provide by new legislation that this exonerating circumstance is not admitted; whereas, in the case of new legislation, making use of this derogation should, however, be subject to a Community stand-still procedure, in order to raise, if possible, the level of protection in a uniform manner throughout the Community;

Whereas, taking into account the legal traditions in most of the Member States, it is inappropriate to set any financial ceiling on the producer's liability without fault; whereas, in so far as there are, however, differing traditions, it seems possible to admit that a Member State may derogate from the principle of unlimited liability by providing a limit for the total liability of the producer for damage resulting from a death or personal injury and caused by identical items with the same defect, provided that this limit is established at a level sufficiently high to guarantee adequate protection of the consumer and the correct functioning of the common market;

Whereas the harmonization resulting from this cannot be total at the present stage, but opens the way towards greater harmonization; whereas it is therefore necessary that the Council receive at regular intervals, reports from the Commission on the application of this Directive, accompanied, as the case may be, by appropriate proposals;

Whereas it is particularly important in this respect that a re-examination be carried out of those parts of the Directive relating to the derogations open to the Member States, at the expiry of a period of sufficient length to gather practical experience on the effects of these derogations on the protection of consumers and on the functioning of the common market.

HAS ADOPTED THIS DIRECTIVE:

Article 1
The producer shall be liable for damage caused by a defect in his product.

Article 2
For the purpose of this Directive 'product' means all movables, with the exception of primary agricultural products and game, even though incorporated into another movable or into an immovable. 'Primary agricultural products' means the products of the soil, of stock-farming and of fisheries, excluding products which have undergone initial

processing. 'Product' includes electricity.

Article 3

1. 'Producer' means the manufacturer of a finished product, the producer of any raw material or the manufacturer of a component part and any person who, by putting his name, trade mark or other distinguishing feature on the product presents himself as its producer.
2. Without prejudice to the liability of the producer, any person who imports into the Community a product for sale, hire, leasing or any form of distribution in the course of his business shall be deemed to be a producer within the meaning of this Directive and shall be responsible as a producer.
3. Where the producer of the product cannot be identified, each supplier of the product shall be treated as its producer unless he informs the injured person, within a reasonable time, of the identity of the producer or of the person who supplied him with the product. The same shall apply, in the case of an imported product, if this product does not indicate the identity of the importer referred to in paragraph 2, even if the name of the producer is indicated.

Article 4

The injured person shall be required to prove the damage, the defect and the causal relationship between defect and damage.

Article 5

Where, as a result of the provisions of this Directive, two or more persons are liable for the same damage, they shall be liable jointly and severally, without prejudice to the provisions of national law concerning the rights of contribution or recourse.

Article 6

1. A product is defective when it does not provide the safety which a person is entitled to expect, taking all circumstances into account, including:
   (a) the presentation of the product;
   (b) the use to which it could reasonably be expected that the product would be put;
   (c) the time when the product was put into circulation.
2. A product shall not be considered defective for the sole reason that a better product is subsequently put into circulation.

Article 7
The producer shall not be liable as a result of this Directive if he proves:
  (a) that he did not put the product into circulation; or
  (b) that, having regard to the circumstances, it is probable that the defect which caused the damage did not exist at the time when the product was put into circulation by him or that this defect came into being afterwards; or
  (c) that the product was neither manufactured by him for sale or any form of distribution for economic purpose nor manufactured or distributed by him in the course of his business; or
      (d) that the defect is due to compliance of the product with mandatory regulations issued by the public authorities; or
  (e) that the state of scientific and technical knowledge at the time when he put the product into circulation was not such as to enable the existence of the defect to be discovered; or
  (f) in the case of a manufacturer of a component, that the defect is attributable to the design of the product in which the component has been fitted or to the instructions given by the manufacturer of the product.

Article 8
1. Without prejudice to the provisions of national law concerning the right of contribution or recourse, the liability of the producer shall not be reduced when the damage is caused both by a defect in product and by the act or omission of a third party.
2. The liability of the producer may be reduced or disallowed when, having regard to all the circumstances, the damage is caused both by a defect in the product and by the fault of the injured person or any person for whom the injured person is responsible.

Article 9
For the purpose of Article l, 'damage' means:
  (a) damage caused by death or by personal injuries;
  (b) damage to, or destruction of, any item of property other than the defective product itself, with a lower threshold of 500 ECU, provided that the item of property:
      (i) is of a type ordinarily intended for private use or consumption, and
      (ii) was used by the injured person mainly for his own private use or consumption.

This Article shall be without prejudice to national provisions relating to non-material damage.

Article 10

1. Member States shall provide in their legislation that a limitation period of three years shall apply to proceedings for the recovery of damages as provided for in this Directive. The limitation period shall begin to run from the day on which the plaintiff became aware, or should reasonably have become aware, of the damage, the defect and the identity of the producer.
2. The laws of Member States regulating suspension or interruption of the limitation period shall not be affected by this Directive.

Article 11

Member States shall provide in their legislation that the rights conferred upon the injured person pursuant to this Directive shall be extinguished upon the expiry of a period of 10 years from the date on which the producer put into circulation the actual product which caused the damage, unless the injured person has in the meantime instituted proceedings against the producer.

Article 12

The liability of the producer arising from this Directive may not, in relation to the injured person, be limited or excluded by a provision limiting his liability or exempting him from liability.

Article 13

This Directive shall not affect any rights which an injured person may have according to the rules of the law of contractual or non-contractual liability or a special liability system existing at the moment when this Directive is notified.

Article 14

This Directive shall not apply to injury or damage arising from nuclear accidents and covered by international conventions ratified by the Member States.

Article 15

1. Each Member State may:
    (a) by way of derogation from Article 2, provide in its legislation that within the meaning of Article 1 of this Directive "product"

also means primary agricultural products and game;

(b) by way of derogation from Article 7 (e), maintain or, subject to the procedure set out in paragraph 2 of this Article, provide in this legislation that the producer shall be liable even if he proves that the state of scientific and technical knowledge at the time when he put the product into circulation was not such as to enable the existence of a defect to be discovered.

2. A Member State wishing to introduce the measure specified in paragraph 1(b) shall communicate the text of the proposed measure to the Commission. The Commission shall inform the other Member States thereof.

The Member State concerned shall hold the proposed measure in abeyance for nine months after the Commission is informed and provided that in the meantime the Commission has not submitted to the Council a proposal amending this Directive on the relevant matter. However, if within three months of receiving the said information, the Commission does not advise the Member State concerned that it intends submitting such a proposal to the Council, the Member State may take the proposed measure immediately.

If the Commission does submit to the Council such a proposal amending this Directive within the aforementioned nine months, the Member State concerned shall hold the proposed measure in abeyance for a further period of 18 months from the date on which the proposal is submitted.

3. Ten years after the date of notification of this Directive, the Commission shall submit to the Council a report on the effect that rulings by the courts as to the application of Article 7(e) and of paragraph 1(b) of this Article have on consumer protection and the functioning of the common market. In the light of this report the Council, acting on a proposal from the Commission and pursuant to the terms of Article 100 of the Treaty, shall decide whether to repeal Article 7(e).

Article 16

1. Any Member State may provide that a producer's total liability for damage resulting from a death or personal injury and caused by identical items with the same defect shall be limited to an amount which may not be less than 70 million ECU.

2. Ten years after the date of notification of this Directive, the Commission shall submit to the Council a report on the effect on consumer protection and the functioning of the common market of

the implementation of the financial limit on liability by those Member States which have used the option provided for in paragraph 1. In the light of this report the Council, acting on a proposal from the Commission and pursuant to the terms of Article 100 of the Treaty, shall decide whether to repeal paragraph 1.

Article 17
This Directive shall not apply to products put into circulation before the date on which the provisions referred to in Article 19 enter into force.

Article 18
1. For the purposes of this Directive, the ECU shall be that defined by Regulation (EEC) No 3180/78 (OJ No L 379, 30. 12. 1978. p.1.), as amended by Regulation (EEC) No 2626/84 (OJ No L 247, 16. 9. 1984. p.1). The equivalent in national currency shall initially be calculated at the rate obtaining on the date of adoption of this Directive.
2. Every five years the Council, acting on a proposal from the Commission, shall examine and, if need be, revise the amounts in this Directive, in the light of economic and monetary trends in the Community.

Article 19
1. Member States shall bring into force, not later than three years from the date of notification of this Directive [30 July 1985] , the laws, regulations and administrative provisions necessary to comply with this Directive. They shall forthwith inform the Commission thereof.
2. The procedure set out in Article 15(2) shall apply from the date of notification of this Directive.

Article 20
Member States shall communicate to the Commission the texts of the main provisions of national law which they subsequently adopt in the field governed by this Directive.

Article 21
Every five years the Commission shall present a report to the Council on the application of this Directive and, if necessary, shall submit appropriate proposals to it.

Article 22
This Directive is addressed to the Member States.

Done at Brussels, 25 July 1985.

Appendix 2

Consumer Protection Act 1987

CHAPTER 43

ARRANGEMENT OF SECTIONS

Consumer Protection Act 1987

1987 CHAPTER 43

An Act to make provision with respect to the liability of persons for damage caused by defective products; to consolidate with amendments the Consumer Safety Act 1978 and the Consumer Safety (Amendment) Act 1986; to make provision with respect to the giving of price indications; to amend Part I of the Health and Safety at Work etc. Act 1974 and sections 31 and 80 of the Explosives Act 1875; to repeal the Trade Descriptions Act 1972 and the Fabrics (Misdescription) Act 1913; and for connected purposes.   [15th May 1987]

BE IT ENACTED by the Queen's most Excellent Majesty, by and with the advice and consent of the Lords Spiritual and Temporal, and Commons, in this present Parliament assembled, and by the authority of the same, as follows:—

PART I

PRODUCT LIABILITY

1.—(1) This Part shall have effect for the purpose of making such provision as is necessary in order to comply with the product liability Directive and shall be construed accordingly.

Purpose and construction of Part I.

(2) In this Part, except in so far as the context otherwise requires—

"agricultural produce" means any produce of the soil, of stock-farming or of fisheries;

"dependant" and "relative" have the same meaning as they have in, respectively, the Fatal Accidents Act 1976 and the Damages (Scotland) Act 1976;

1976 c. 30.
1976 c. 13.

"producer", in relation to a product, means—

(a) the person who manufactured it;

(b) in the case of a substance which has not been manufactured but has been won or abstracted, the person who won or abstracted it;

(c) in the case of a product which has not been manufactured, won or abstracted but essential characteristics of which are attributable to an industrial or other process having been carried out (for example, in relation to agricultural produce), the person who carried out that process;

"product" means any goods or electricity and (subject to subsection (3) below) includes a product which is comprised in another product, whether by virtue of being a component part or raw material or otherwise; and

"the product liability Directive" means the Directive of the Council of the European Communities, dated 25th July 1985, (No. 85/374/EEC) on the approximation of the laws, regulations and administrative provisions of the member States concerning liability for defective products.

(3) For the purposes of this Part a person who supplies any product in which products are comprised, whether by virtue of being component parts or raw materials or otherwise, shall not be treated by reason only of his supply of that product as supplying any of the products so comprised.

Liability for defective products.

2.—(1) Subject to the following provisions of this Part, where any damage is caused wholly or partly by a defect in a product, every person to whom subsection (2) below applies shall be liable for the damage.

(2) This subsection applies to—

(a) the producer of the product;

(b) any person who, by putting his name on the product or using a trade mark or other distinguishing mark in relation to the product, has held himself out to be the producer of the product;

(c) any person who has imported the product into a member State from a place outside the member States in order, in the course of any business of his, to supply it to another.

(3) Subject as aforesaid, where any damage is caused wholly or partly by a defect in a product, any person who supplied the product (whether to the person who suffered the damage, to the producer of any product in which the product in question is comprised or to any other person) shall be liable for the damage if—

(a) the person who suffered the damage requests the supplier to identify one or more of the persons (whether still in existence or not) to whom subsection (2) above applies in relation to the product;

(b) that request is made within a reasonable period after the damage occurs and at a time when it is not reasonably practicable for the person making the request to identify all those persons; and

(c) the supplier fails, within a reasonable period after receiving the request, either to comply with the request or to identify the person who supplied the product to him.

(4) Neither subsection (2) nor subsection (3) above shall apply to a person in respect of any defect in any game or agricultural produce if the only supply of the game or produce by that person to another was at a time when it had not undergone an industrial process.

(5) Where two or more persons are liable by virtue of this Part for the same damage, their liability shall be joint and several.

(6) This section shall be without prejudice to any liability arising otherwise than by virtue of this Part.

3.—(1) Subject to the following provisions of this section, there is a defect in a product for the purposes of this Part if the safety of the product is not such as persons generally are entitled to expect; and for those purposes "safety", in relation to a product, shall include safety with respect to products comprised in that product and safety in the context of risks of damage to property, as well as in the context of risks of death or personal injury.

(2) In determining for the purposes of subsection (1) above what persons generally are entitled to expect in relation to a product all the circumstances shall be taken into account, including—

- (a) the manner in which, and purposes for which, the product has been marketed, its get-up, the use of any mark in relation to the product and any instructions for, or warnings with respect to, doing or refraining from doing anything with or in relation to the product;

- (b) what might reasonably be expected to be done with or in relation to the product; and

- (c) the time when the product was supplied by its producer to another;

and nothing in this section shall require a defect to be inferred from the fact alone that the safety of a product which is supplied after that time is greater than the safety of the product in question.

4.—(1) In any civil proceedings by virtue of this Part against any person ("the person proceeded against") in respect of a defect in a product it shall be a defence for him to show—

- (a) that the defect is attributable to compliance with any requirement imposed by or under any enactment or with any Community obligation; or

- (b) that the person proceeded against did not at any time supply the product to another; or

- (c) that the following conditions are satisfied, that is to say—

    (i) that the only supply of the product to another by the person proceeded against was otherwise than in the course of a business of that person's; and

    (ii) that section 2(2) above does not apply to that person or applies to him by virtue only of things done otherwise than with a view to profit; or

- (d) that the defect did not exist in the product at the relevant time; or

- (e) that the state of scientific and technical knowledge at the relevant time was not such that a producer of products of the same description as the product in question might be expected to have discovered the defect if it had existed in his products while they were under his control; or

141

(f) that the defect—

(i) constituted a defect in a product ("the subsequent product") in which the product in question had been comprised; and

(ii) was wholly attributable to the design of the subsequent product or to compliance by the producer of the product in question with instructions given by the producer of the subsequent product.

(2) In this section "the relevant time", in relation to electricity, means the time at which it was generated, being a time before it was transmitted or distributed, and in relation to any other product, means—

(a) if the person proceeded against is a person to whom subsection (2) of section 2 above applies in relation to the product, the time when he supplied the product to another;

(b) if that subsection does not apply to that person in relation to the product, the time when the product was last supplied by a person to whom that subsection does apply in relation to the product.

Damage giving rise to liability.

5.—(1) Subject to the following provisions of this section, in this Part "damage" means death or personal injury or any loss of or damage to any property (including land).

(2) A person shall not be liable under section 2 above in respect of any defect in a product for the loss of or any damage to the product itself or for the loss of or any damage to the whole or any part of any product which has been supplied with the product in question comprised in it.

(3) A person shall not be liable under section 2 above for any loss of or damage to any property which, at the time it is lost or damaged, is not—

(a) of a description of property ordinarily intended for private use, occupation or consumption; and

(b) intended by the person suffering the loss or damage mainly for his own private use, occupation or consumption.

(4) No damages shall be awarded to any person by virtue of this Part in respect of any loss of or damage to any property if the amount which would fall to be so awarded to that person, apart from this subsection and any liability for interest, does not exceed £275.

(5) In determining for the purposes of this Part who has suffered any loss of or damage to property and when any such loss or damage occurred, the loss or damage shall be regarded as having occurred at the earliest time at which a person with an interest in the property had knowledge of the material facts about the loss or damage.

(6) For the purposes of subsection (5) above the material facts about any loss of or damage to any property are such facts about the loss or damage as would lead a reasonable person with an interest in the property to consider the loss or damage sufficiently serious to justify his instituting proceedings for damages against a defendant who did not dispute liability and was able to satisfy a judgment.

(7) For the purposes of subsection (5) above a person's knowledge includes knowledge which he might reasonably have been expected to acquire—

(a) from facts observable or ascertainable by him; or

(b) from facts ascertainable by him with the help of appropriate expert advice which it is reasonable for him to seek;

but a person shall not be taken by virtue of this subsection to have knowledge of a fact ascertainable by him only with the help of expert advice unless he has failed to take all reasonable steps to obtain (and, where appropriate, to act on) that advice.

(8) Subsections (5) to (7) above shall not extend to Scotland.

6.—(1) Any damage for which a person is liable under section 2 above shall be deemed to have been caused—

Application of certain enactments etc.
1976 c. 30.

(a) for the purposes of the Fatal Accidents Act 1976, by that person's wrongful act, neglect or default;

(b) for the purposes of section 3 of the Law Reform (Miscellaneous Provisions) (Scotland) Act 1940 (contribution among joint wrongdoers), by that person's wrongful act or negligent act or omission;

1940 c. 42.

(c) for the purposes of section 1 of the Damages (Scotland) Act 1976 (rights of relatives of a deceased), by that person's act or omission; and

1976 c. 13.

(d) for the purposes of Part II of the Administration of Justice Act 1982 (damages for personal injuries, etc.—Scotland), by an act or omission giving rise to liability in that person to pay damages.

1982 c. 53.

(2) Where—

(a) a person's death is caused wholly or partly by a defect in a product, or a person dies after suffering damage which has been so caused;

(b) a request such as mentioned in paragraph (a) of subsection (3) of section 2 above is made to a supplier of the product by that person's personal representatives or, in the case of a person whose death is caused wholly or partly by the defect, by any dependant or relative of that person; and

(c) the conditions specified in paragraphs (b) and (c) of that subsection are satisfied in relation to that request,

this Part shall have effect for the purposes of the Law Reform (Miscellaneous Provisions) Act 1934, the Fatal Accidents Act 1976 and the Damages (Scotland) Act 1976 as if liability of the supplier to that person under that subsection did not depend on that person having requested the supplier to identify certain persons or on the said conditions having been satisified in relation to a request made by that person.

1934 c. 41.

(3) Section 1 of the Congenital Disabilities (Civil Liability) Act 1976 shall have effect for the purposes of this Part as if—

1976 c. 28.

(a) a person were answerable to a child in respect of an occurrence caused wholly or partly by a defect in a product if he is or has been liable under section 2 above in respect of any effect of the occurrence on a parent of the child, or would be so liable if the occurrence caused a parent of the child to suffer damage;

(b) the provisions of this Part relating to liability under section 2 above applied in relation to liability by virtue of paragraph (a) above under the said section 1; and

(c)   subsection (6) of the said section 1 (exclusion of liability) were omitted.

(4) Where any damage is caused partly by a defect in a product and partly by the fault of the person suffering the damage, the Law Reform (Contributory Negligence) Act 1945 and section 5 of the Fatal Accidents Act 1976 (contributory negligence) shall have effect as if the defect were the fault of every person liable by virtue of this Part for the damage caused by the defect.

1945 c. 28.
1976 c.30.

(5) In subsection (4) above "fault" has the same meaning as in the said Act of 1945.

(6) Schedule 1 to this Act shall have effect for the purpose of amending the Limitation Act 1980 and the Prescription and Limitation (Scotland) Act 1973 in their application in relation to the bringing of actions by virtue of this Part.

1980 c. 58.
1973 c. 52.

(7) It is hereby declared that liability by virtue of this Part is to be treated as liability in tort for the purposes of any enactment conferring jurisdiction on any court with respect to any matter.

(8) Nothing in this Part shall prejudice the operation of section 12 of the Nuclear Installations Act 1965 (rights to compensation for certain breaches of duties confined to rights under that Act).

1965 c. 57.

Prohibition on exclusions from liability.

7. The liability of a person by virtue of this Part to a person who has suffered damage caused wholly or partly by a defect in a product, or to a dependant or relative of such a person, shall not be limited or excluded by any contract term, by any notice or by any other provision.

Power to modify Part I.

8.—(1) Her Majesty may by Order in Council make such modifications of this Part and of any other enactment (including an enactment contained in the following Parts of this Act, or in an Act passed after this Act) as appear to Her Majesty in Council to be necessary or expedient in consequence of any modification of the product liability Directive which is made at any time after the passing of this Act.

(2) An Order in Council under subsection (1) above shall not be submitted to Her Majesty in Council unless a draft of the Order has been laid before, and approved by a resolution of, each House of Parliament.

Application of Part I to Crown.

9.—(1) Subject to subsection (2) below, this Part shall bind the Crown.

(2) The Crown shall not, as regards the Crown's liability by virtue of this Part, be bound by this Part further than the Crown is made liable in tort or in reparation under the Crown Proceedings Act 1947, as that Act has effect from time to time.

1947 c. 44.

PART II

CONSUMER SAFETY

The general safety requirement.

10.—(1) A person shall be guilty of an offence if he—

(a)   supplies any consumer goods which fail to comply with the general safety requirement;

(b)   offers or agrees to supply any such goods; or

(c) exposes or possesses any such goods for supply.

(2) For the purposes of this section consumer goods fail to comply with the general safety requirement if they are not reasonably safe having regard to all the circumstances, including—

- (a) the manner in which, and purposes for which, the goods are being or would be marketed, the get-up of the goods, the use of any mark in relation to the goods and any instructions or warnings which are given or would be given with respect to the keeping, use or consumption of the goods;

- (b) any standards of safety published by any person either for goods of a description which applies to the goods in question or for matters relating to goods of that description; and

- (c) the existence of any means by which it would have been reasonable (taking into account the cost, likelihood and extent of any improvement) for the goods to have been made safer.

(3) For the purposes of this section consumer goods shall not be regarded as failing to comply with the general safety requirement in respect of—

- (a) anything which is shown to be attributable to compliance with any requirement imposed by or under any enactment or with any Community obligation;

- (b) any failure to do more in relation to any matter than is required by—

    (i) any safety regulations imposing requirements with respect to that matter;

    (ii) any standards of safety approved for the purposes of this subsection by or under any such regulations and imposing requirements with respect to that matter;

    (iii) any provision of any enactment or subordinate legislation imposing such requirements with respect to that matter as are designated for the purposes of this subsection by any such regulations.

(4) In any proceedings against any person for an offence under this section in respect of any goods it shall be a defence for that person to show—

- (a) that he reasonably believed that the goods would not be used or consumed in the United Kingdom; or

- (b) that the following conditions are satisfied, that is to say–

    (i) that he supplied the goods, offered or agreed to supply them or, as the case may be, exposed or possessed them for supply in the course of carrying on a retail business; and

    (ii) that, at the time he supplied the goods or offered or agreed to supply them or exposed or possessed them for supply, he neither knew nor had reasonable grounds for believing that the goods failed to comply with the general safety requirement; or

- (c) that the terms on which he supplied the goods or agreed or offered to supply them or, in the case of goods which he exposed or possessed for supply, the terms on which he intended to supply them—

(i) indicated that the goods were not supplied or to be supplied as new goods; and

(ii) provided for, or contemplated, the acquisition of an interest in the goods by the persons supplied or to be supplied.

(5) For the purposes of subsection (4)(b) above goods are supplied in the course of carrying on a retail business if—

(a) whether or not they are themselves acquired for a person's private use or consumption, they are supplied in the course of carrying on a business of making a supply of consumer goods available to persons who generally acquire them for private use or consumption; and

(b) the descriptions of goods the supply of which is made available in the course of that business do not, to a significant extent, include manufactured or imported goods which have not previously been supplied in the United Kingdom.

(6) A person guilty of an offence under this section shall be liable on summary conviction to imprisonment for a term not exceeding six months or to a fine not exceeding level 5 on the standard scale or to both.

(7) In this section "consumer goods" means any goods which are ordinarily intended for private use or consumption, not being—

(a) growing crops or things comprised in land by virtue of being attached to it;

(b) water, food, feeding stuff or fertiliser;

(c) gas which is, is to be or has been supplied by a person authorised to supply it by or under section 6, 7 or 8 of the Gas Act 1986 (authorisation of supply of gas through pipes);

1986 c. 44.

(d) aircraft (other than hang-gliders) or motor vehicles;

(e) controlled drugs or licensed medicinal products;

(f) tobacco.

Safety regulations.

11.—(1) The Secretary of State may by regulations under this section ("safety regulations") make such provision as he considers appropriate for the purposes of section 10(3) above and for the purpose of securing—

(a) that goods to which this section applies are safe;

(b) that goods to which this section applies which are unsafe, or would be unsafe in the hands of persons of a particular description, are not made available to persons generally or, as the case may be, to persons of that description; and

(c) that appropriate information is, and inappropriate information is not, provided in relation to goods to which this section applies.

(2) Without prejudice to the generality of subsection (1) above, safety regulations may contain provision—

(a) with respect to the composition or contents, design, construction, finish or packing of goods to which this section applies, with respect to standards for such goods and with respect to other matters relating to such goods;

(b) with respect to the giving, refusal, alteration or cancellation of approvals of such goods, of descriptions of such goods or of standards for such goods;

(c) with respect to the conditions that may be attached to any approval given under the regulations;

(d) for requiring such fees as may be determined by or under the regulations to be paid on the giving or alteration of any approval under the regulations and on the making of an application for such an approval or alteration;

(e) with respect to appeals against refusals, alterations and cancellations of approvals given under the regulations and against the conditions contained in such approvals;

(f) for requiring goods to which this section applies to be approved under the regulations or to conform to the requirements of the regulations or to descriptions or standards specified in or approved by or under the regulations;

(g) with respect to the testing or inspection of goods to which this section applies (including provision for determining the standards to be applied in carrying out any test or inspection);

(h) with respect to the ways of dealing with goods of which some or all do not satisfy a test required by or under the regulations or a standard connected with a procedure so required;

(i) for requiring a mark, warning or instruction or any other information relating to goods to be put on or to accompany the goods or to be used or provided in some other manner in relation to the goods, and for securing that inappropriate information is not given in relation to goods either by means of misleading marks or otherwise;

(j) for prohibiting persons from supplying, or from offering to supply, agreeing to supply, exposing for supply or possessing for supply, goods to which this section applies and component parts and raw materials for such goods;

(k) for requiring information to be given to any such person as may be determined by or under the regulations for the purpose of enabling that person to exercise any function conferred on him by the regulations.

(3) Without prejudice as aforesaid, safety regulations may contain provision—

(a) for requiring persons on whom functions are conferred by or under section 27 below to have regard, in exercising their functions so far as relating to any provision of safety regulations, to matters specified in a direction issued by the Secretary of State with respect to that provision;

(b) for securing that a person shall not be guilty of an offence under section 12 below unless it is shown that the goods in question do not conform to a particular standard;

(c) for securing that proceedings for such an offence are not brought in England and Wales except by or with the consent of the Secretary of State or the Director of Public Prosecutions;

(d) for securing that proceedings for such an offence are not brought in Northern Ireland except by or with the consent of the Secretary of State or the Director of Public Prosecutions for Northern Ireland;

(e) for enabling a magistrates' court in England and Wales or Northern Ireland to try an information or, in Northern Ireland, a complaint in respect of such an offence if the information was laid or the complaint made within twelve months from the time when the offence was committed;

(f) for enabling summary proceedings for such an offence to be brought in Scotland at any time within twelve months from the time when the offence was committed; and

(g) for determining the persons by whom, and the manner in which, anything required to be done by or under the regulations is to be done.

(4) Safety regulations shall not provide for any contravention of the regulations to be an offence.

(5) Where the Secretary of State proposes to make safety regulations it shall be his duty before he makes them—

(a) to consult such organisations as appear to him to be representative of interests substantially affected by the proposal;

(b) to consult such other persons as he considers appropriate; and

(c) in the case of proposed regulations relating to goods suitable for use at work, to consult the Health and Safety Commission in relation to the application of the proposed regulations to Great Britain;

but the preceding provisions of this subsection shall not apply in the case of regulations which provide for the regulations to cease to have effect at the end of a period of not more than twelve months beginning with the day on which they come into force and which contain a statement that it appears to the Secretary of State that the need to protect the public requires that the regulations should be made without delay.

(6) The power to make safety regulations shall be exercisable by statutory instrument subject to annulment in pursuance of a resolution of either House of Parliament and shall include power—

(a) to make different provision for different cases; and

(b) to make such supplemental, consequential and transitional provision as the Secretary of State considers appropriate.

(7) This section applies to any goods other than—

(a) growing crops and things comprised in land by virtue of being attached to it;

(b) water, food, feeding stuff and fertiliser;

1986 c. 44.   (c) gas which is, is to be or has been supplied by a person authorised to supply it by or under section 6, 7 or 8 of the Gas Act 1986 (authorisation of supply of gas through pipes);

(d) controlled drugs and licensed medicinal products.

Offences against the safety regulations.   **12.**—(1) Where safety regulations prohibit a person from supplying or offering or agreeing to supply any goods or from exposing or possessing any goods for supply, that person shall be guilty of an offence if he contravenes the prohibition.

(2) Where safety regulations require a person who makes or processes any goods in the course of carrying on a business—

(a) to carry out a particular test or use a particular procedure in connection with the making or processing of the goods with a view to ascertaining whether the goods satisfy any requirements of such regulations; or

(b) to deal or not to deal in a particular way with a quantity of the goods of which the whole or part does not satisfy such a test or does not satisfy standards connected with such a procedure,

that person shall be guilty of an offence if he does not comply with the requirement.

(3) If a person contravenes a provision of safety regulations which prohibits or requires the provision, by means of a mark or otherwise, of information of a particular kind in relation to goods, he shall be guilty of an offence.

(4) Where safety regulations require any person to give information to another for the purpose of enabling that other to exercise any function, that person shall be guilty of an offence if—

(a) he fails without reasonable cause to comply with the requirement; or

(b) in giving the information which is required of him—

(i) he makes any statement which he knows is false in a material particular; or

(ii) he recklessly makes any statement which is false in a material particular.

(5) A person guilty of an offence under this section shall be liable on summary conviction to imprisonment for a term not exceeding six months or to a fine not exceeding level 5 on the standard scale or to both.

13.—(1) The Secretary of State may—

(a) serve on any person a notice ("a prohibition notice") prohibiting that person, except with the consent of the Secretary of State, from supplying, or from offering to supply, agreeing to supply, exposing for supply or possessing for supply, any relevant goods which the Secretary of State considers are unsafe and which are described in the notice;

Prohibition notices and notices to warn.

(b) serve on any person a notice ("a notice to warn") requiring that person at his own expense to publish, in a form and manner and on occasions specified in the notice, a warning about any relevant goods which the Secretary of State considers are unsafe, which that person supplies or has supplied and which are described in the notice.

(2) Schedule 2 to this Act shall have effect with respect to prohibition notices and notices to warn; and the Secretary of State may by regulations make provision specifying the manner in which information is to be given to any person under that Schedule.

(3) A consent given by the Secretary of State for the purposes of a prohibition notice may impose such conditions on the doing of anything for which the consent is required as the Secretary of State considers appropriate.

(4) A person who contravenes a prohibition notice or a notice to warn shall be guilty of an offence and liable on summary conviction to imprisonment for a term not exceeding six months or to a fine not exceeding level 5 on the standard scale or to both.

(5) The power to make regulations under subsection (2) above shall be exercisable by statutory instrument subject to annulment in pursuance of a resolution of either House of Parliament and shall include power—

    (a) to make different provision for different cases; and

    (b) to make such supplemental, consequential and transitional provision as the Secretary of State considers appropriate.

(6) In this section "relevant goods" means—

    (a) in relation to a prohibition notice, any goods to which section 11 above applies; and

    (b) in relation to a notice to warn, any goods to which that section applies or any growing crops or things comprised in land by virtue of being attached to it.

Suspension
notices.

14.—(1) Where an enforcement authority has reasonable grounds for suspecting that any safety provision has been contravened in relation to any goods, the authority may serve a notice ("a suspension notice") prohibiting the person on whom it is served, for such period ending not more than six months after the date of the notice as is specified therein, from doing any of the following things without the consent of the authority, that is to say, supplying the goods, offering to supply them, agreeing to supply them or exposing them for supply.

(2) A suspension notice served by an enforcement authority in respect of any goods shall—

    (a) describe the goods in a manner sufficient to identify them;

    (b) set out the grounds on which the authority suspects that a safety provision has been contravened in relation to the goods; and

    (c) state that, and the manner in which, the person on whom the notice is served may appeal against the notice under section 15 below.

(3) A suspension notice served by an enforcement authority for the purpose of prohibiting a person for any period from doing the things mentioned in subsection (1) above in relation to any goods may also require that person to keep the authority informed of the whereabouts throughout that period of any of those goods in which he has an interest.

(4) Where a suspension notice has been served on any person in respect of any goods, no further such notice shall be served on that person in respect of the same goods unless—

    (a) proceedings against that person for an offence in respect of a contravention in relation to the goods of a safety provision (not being an offence under this section); or

    (b) proceedings for the forfeiture of the goods under section 16 or 17 below,

are pending at the end of the period specified in the first-mentioned notice.

(5) A consent given by an enforcement authority for the purposes of subsection (1) above may impose such conditions on the doing of anything for which the consent is required as the authority considers appropriate.

(6) Any person who contravenes a suspension notice shall be guilty of an offence and liable on summary conviction to imprisonment for a term not exceeding six months or to a fine not exceeding level 5 on the standard scale or to both.

(7) Where an enforcement authority serves a suspension notice in respect of any goods, the authority shall be liable to pay compensation to any person having an interest in the goods in respect of any loss or damage caused by reason of the service of the notice if—

    (a) there has been no contravention in relation to the goods of any safety provision; and

    (b) the exercise of the power is not attributable to any neglect or default by that person.

(8) Any disputed question as to the right to or the amount of any compensation payable under this section shall be determined by arbitration or, in Scotland, by a single arbiter appointed, failing agreement between the parties, by the sheriff.

15.—(1) Any person having an interest in any goods in respect of which a suspension notice is for the time being in force may apply for an order setting aside the notice.

(2) An application under this section may be made—

    (a) to any magistrates' court in which proceedings have been brought in England and Wales or Northern Ireland—

        (i) for an offence in respect of a contravention in relation to the goods of any safety provision; or

        (ii) for the forfeiture of the goods under section 16 below;

    (b) where no such proceedings have been so brought, by way of complaint to a magistrates' court; or

    (c) in Scotland, by summary application to the sheriff.

(3) On an application under this section to a magistrates' court in England and Wales or Northern Ireland the court shall make an order setting aside the suspension notice only if the court is satisfied that there has been no contravention in relation to the goods of any safety provision.

(4) On an application under this section to the sheriff he shall make an order setting aside the suspension notice only if he is satisfied that at the date of making the order—

    (a) proceedings for an offence in respect of a contravention in relation to the goods of any safety provision; or

    (b) proceedings for the forfeiture of the goods under section 17 below,

have not been brought or, having been brought, have been concluded.

(5) Any person aggrieved by an order made under this section by a magistrates' court in England and Wales or Northern Ireland, or by a decision of such a court not to make such an order, may appeal against that order or decision—

    (a) in England and Wales, to the Crown Court;

(b) in Northern Ireland, to the county court;

and an order so made may contain such provision as appears to the court to be appropriate for delaying the coming into force of the order pending the making and determination of any appeal (including any application under section 111 of the Magistrates' Courts Act 1980 or Article 146 of the Magistrates' Courts (Northern Ireland) Order 1981 (statement of case)).

16.—(1) An enforcement authority in England and Wales or Northern Ireland may apply under this section for an order for the forfeiture of any goods on the grounds that there has been a contravention in relation to the goods of a safety provision.

(2) An application under this section may be made—

(a) where proceedings have been brought in a magistrates' court for an offence in respect of a contravention in relation to some or all of the goods of any safety provision, to that court;

(b) where an application with respect to some or all of the goods has been made to a magistrates' court under section 15 above or section 33 below, to that court; and

(c) where no application for the forfeiture of the goods has been made under paragraph (a) or (b) above, by way of complaint to a magistrates' court.

(3) On an application under this section the court shall make an order for the forfeiture of any goods only if it is satisfied that there has been a contravention in relation to the goods of a safety provision.

(4) For the avoidance of doubt it is declared that a court may infer for the purposes of this section that there has been a contravention in relation to any goods of a safety provision if it is satisfied that any such provision has been contravened in relation to goods which are representative of those goods (whether by reason of being of the same design or part of the same consignment or batch or otherwise).

(5) Any person aggrieved by an order made under this section by a magistrates' court, or by a decision of such a court not to make such an order, may appeal against that order or decision—

(a) in England and Wales, to the Crown Court;

(b) in Northern Ireland, to the county court;

and an order so made may contain such provision as appears to the court to be appropriate for delaying the coming into force of the order pending the making and determination of any appeal (including any application under section 111 of the Magistrates' Courts Act 1980 or Article 146 of the Magistrates' Courts (Northern Ireland) Order 1981 (statement of case)).

(6) Subject to subsection (7) below, where any goods are forfeited under this section they shall be destroyed in accordance with such directions as the court may give.

(7) On making an order under this section a magistrates' court may, if it considers it appropriate to do so, direct that the goods to which the order relates shall (instead of being destroyed) be released, to such person as the court may specify, on condition that that person—

(a) does not supply those goods to any person otherwise than as mentioned in section 46(7)(a) or (b) below; and

(b) complies with any order to pay costs or expenses (including any order under section 35 below) which has been made against that person in the proceedings for the order for forfeiture.

17.—(1) In Scotland a sheriff may make an order for forfeiture of any goods in relation to which there has been a contravention of a safety provision—

(a) on an application by the procurator-fiscal made in the manner specified in section 310 of the Criminal Procedure (Scotland) Act 1975; or

(b) where a person is convicted of any offence in respect of any such contravention, in addition to any other penalty which the sheriff may impose.

(2) The procurator-fiscal making an application under subsection (1)(a) above shall serve on any person appearing to him to be the owner of, or otherwise to have an interest in, the goods to which the application relates a copy of the application, together with a notice giving him the opportunity to appear at the hearing of the application to show cause why the goods should not be forfeited.

(3) Service under subsection (2) above shall be carried out, and such service may be proved, in the manner specified for citation of an accused in summary proceedings under the Criminal Procedure (Scotland) Act 1975.

(4) Any person upon whom notice is served under subsection (2) above and any other person claiming to be the owner of, or otherwise to have an interest in, goods to which an application under this section relates shall be entitled to appear at the hearing of the application to show cause why the goods should not be forfeited.

(5) The sheriff shall not make an order following an application under subsection (1)(a) above—

(a) if any person on whom notice is served under subsection (2) above does not appear, unless service of the notice on that person is proved; or

(b) if no notice under subsection (2) above has been served, unless the court is satisfied that in the circumstances it was reasonable not to serve notice on any person.

(6) The sheriff shall make an order under this section only if he is satisfied that there has been a contravention in relation to those goods of a safety provision.

(7) For the avoidance of doubt it is declared that the sheriff may infer for the purposes of this section that there has been a contravention in relation to any goods of a safety provision if he is satisfied that any such provision has been contravened in relation to any goods which are representative of those goods (whether by reason of being of the same design or part of the same consignment or batch or otherwise).

(8) Where an order for the forfeiture of any goods is made following an application by the procurator-fiscal under subsection (1)(a) above, any person who appeared, or was entitled to appear, to show cause why goods should not be forfeited may, within twenty-one days of the making of the

B

order, appeal to the High Court by Bill of Suspension on the ground of an alleged miscarriage of justice; and section 452(4)(a) to (e) of the Criminal Procedure (Scotland) Act 1975 shall apply to an appeal under this subsection as it applies to a stated case under Part II of that Act.

(9) An order following an application under subsection (1)(a) above shall not take effect—

(a) until the end of the period of twenty-one days beginning with the day after the day on which the order is made; or

(b) if an appeal is made under subsection (8) above within that period, until the appeal is determined or abandoned.

(10) An order under subsection (1)(b) above shall not take effect—

(a) until the end of the period within which an appeal against the order could be brought under the Criminal Procedure (Scotland) Act 1975; or

(b) if an appeal is made within that period, until the appeal is determined or abandoned.

(11) Subject to subsection (12) below, goods forfeited under this section shall be destroyed in accordance with such directions as the sheriff may give.

(12) If he thinks fit, the sheriff may direct that the goods be released, to such person as he may specify, on condition that that person does not supply those goods to any other person otherwise than as mentioned in section 46(7)(a) or (b) below.

Power to obtain
information.

18.—(1) If the Secretary of State considers that, for the purpose of deciding whether—

(a) to make, vary or revoke any safety regulations; or

(b) to serve, vary or revoke a prohibition notice; or

(c) to serve or revoke a notice to warn,

he requires information which another person is likely to be able to furnish, the Secretary of State may serve on the other person a notice under this section.

(2) A notice served on any person under this section may require that person—

(a) to furnish to the Secretary of State, within a period specified in the notice, such information as is so specified;

(b) to produce such records as are specified in the notice at a time and place so specified and to permit a person appointed by the Secretary of State for the purpose to take copies of the records at that time and place.

(3) A person shall be guilty of an offence if he—

(a) fails, without reasonable cause, to comply with a notice served on him under this section; or

(b) in purporting to comply with a requirement which by virtue of paragraph (a) of subsection (2) above is contained in such a notice—

(i) furnishes information which he knows is false in a material particular; or

(ii) recklessly furnishes information which is false in a material particular.

(4) A person guilty of an offence under subsection (3) above shall—

(a) in the case of an offence under paragraph (a) of that subsection, be liable on summary conviction to a fine not exceeding level 5 on the standard scale; and

(b) in the case of an offence under paragraph (b) of that subsection be liable—

(i) on conviction on indictment, to a fine;

(ii) on summary conviction, to a fine not exceeding the statutory maximum.

19.—(1) In this Part—

"controlled drug" means a controlled drug within the meaning of the Misuse of Drugs Act 1971;

"feeding stuff" and "fertiliser" have the same meanings as in Part IV of the Agriculture Act 1970;

"food" does not include anything containing tobacco but, subject to that, has the same meaning as in the Food Act 1984 or, in relation to Northern Ireland, the same meaning as in the Food and Drugs Act (Northern Ireland) 1958;

"licensed medicinal product" means—

(a) any medicinal product within the meaning of the Medicines Act 1968 in respect of which a product licence within the meaning of that Act is for the time being in force; or

(b) any other article or substance in respect of which any such licence is for the time being in force in pursuance of an order under section 104 or 105 of that Act (application of Act to other articles and substances);

"safe", in relation to any goods, means such that there is no risk, or no risk apart from one reduced to a minimum, that any of the following will (whether immediately or after a definite or indefinite period) cause the death of, or any personal injury to, any person whatsoever, that is to say—

(a) the goods;

(b) the keeping, use or consumption of the goods;

(c) the assembly of any of the goods which are, or are to be, supplied unassembled;

(d) any emission or leakage from the goods or, as a result of the keeping, use or consumption of the goods, from anything else; or

(e) reliance on the accuracy of any measurement, calculation or other reading made by or by means of the goods,

and "safer" and "unsafe" shall be construed accordingly;

"tobacco" includes any tobacco product within the meaning of the Tobacco Products Duty Act 1979 and any article or substance containing tobacco and intended for oral or nasal use.

(2) In the definition of "safe" in subsection (1) above, references to the keeping, use or consumption of any goods are references to—

(a)   the keeping, use or consumption of the goods by the persons by whom, and in all or any of the ways or circumstances in which, they might reasonably be expected to be kept, used or consumed; and

(b)   the keeping, use or consumption of the goods either alone or in conjunction with other goods in conjunction with which they might reasonably be expected to be kept, used or consumed.

Part III

Misleading Price Indications

Offence of giving misleading indication.

20.—(1) Subject to the following provisions of this Part, a person shall be guilty of an offence if, in the course of any business of his, he gives (by any means whatever) to any consumers an indication which is misleading as to the price at which any goods, services, accommodation or facilities are available (whether generally or from particular persons).

(2) Subject as aforesaid, a person shall be guilty of an offence if—

(a)   in the course of any business of his, he has given an indication to any consumers which, after it was given, has become misleading as mentioned in subsection (1) above; and

(b)   some or all of those consumers might reasonably be expected to rely on the indication at a time after it has become misleading; and

(c)   he fails to take all such steps as are reasonable to prevent those consumers from relying on the indication.

(3) For the purposes of this section it shall be immaterial—

(a)   whether the person who gives or gave the indication is or was acting on his own behalf or on behalf of another;

(b)   whether or not that person is the person, or included among the persons, from whom the goods, services, accommodation or facilities are available; and

(c)   whether the indication is or has become misleading in relation to all the consumers to whom it is or was given or only in relation to some of them.

(4) A person guilty of an offence under subsection (1) or (2) above shall be liable—

(a)   on conviction on indictment, to a fine;

(b)   on summary conviction, to a fine not exceeding the statutory maximum.

(5) No prosecution for an offence under subsection (1) or (2) above shall be brought after whichever is the earlier of the following, that is to say—

(a)   the end of the period of three years beginning with the day on which the offence was committed; and

(b)   the end of the period of one year beginning with the day on which the person bringing the prosecution discovered that the offence had been committed.

(6) In this Part—

"consumer"—

(a) in relation to any goods, means any person who might wish to be supplied with the goods for his own private use or consumption;

(b) in relation to any services or facilities, means any person who might wish to be provided with the services or facilities otherwise than for the purposes of any business of his; and

(c) in relation to any accommodation, means any person who might wish to occupy the accommodation otherwise than for the purposes of any business of his;

"price", in relation to any goods, services, accommodation or facilities, means—

(a) the aggregate of the sums required to be paid by a consumer for or otherwise in respect of the supply of the goods or the provision of the services, accommodation or facilities; or

(b) except in section 21 below, any method which will be or has been applied for the purpose of determining that aggregate.

21.—(1) For the purposes of section 20 above an indication given to any consumers is misleading as to a price if what is conveyed by the indication, or what those consumers might reasonably be expected to infer from the indication or any omission from it, includes any of the following, that is to say—

(a) that the price is less than in fact it is;

(b) that the applicability of the price does not depend on facts or circumstances on which its applicability does in fact depend;

(c) that the price covers matters in respect of which an additional charge is in fact made;

(d) that a person who in fact has no such expectation—

(i) expects the price to be increased or reduced (whether or not at a particular time or by a particular amount); or

(ii) expects the price, or the price as increased or reduced, to be maintained (whether or not for a particular period); or

(e) that the facts or circumstances by reference to which the consumers might reasonably be expected to judge the validity of any relevant comparison made or implied by the indication are not what in fact they are.

(2) For the purposes of section 20 above, an indication given to any consumers is misleading as to a method of determining a price if what is conveyed by the indication, or what those consumers might reasonably be expected to infer from the indication or any omission from it, includes any of the following, that is to say—

(a) that the method is not what in fact it is;

(b) that the applicability of the method does not depend on facts or circumstances on which its applicability does in fact depend;

(c) that the method takes into account matters in respect of which an additional charge will in fact be made;

(d) that a person who in fact has no such expectation—

    (i) expects the method to be altered (whether or not at a particular time or in a particular respect); or

    (ii) expects the method, or that method as altered, to remain unaltered (whether or not for a particular period); or

(e) that the facts or circumstances by reference to which the consumers might reasonably be expected to judge the validity of any relevant comparison made or implied by the indication are not what in fact they are.

(3) For the purposes of subsections (1)(e) and (2)(e) above a comparison is a relevant comparison in relation to a price or method of determining a price if it is made between that price or that method, or any price which has been or may be determined by that method, and—

(a) any price or value which is stated or implied to be, to have been or to be likely to be attributed or attributable to the goods, services, accommodation or facilities in question or to any other goods, services, accommodation or facilities; or

(b) any method, or other method, which is stated or implied to be, to have been or to be likely to be applied or applicable for the determination of the price or value of the goods, services, accommodation or facilities in question or of the price or value of any other goods, services, accommodation or facilities.

Application to
provision of
services and
facilities.

22.—(1) Subject to the following provisions of this section, references in this Part to services or facilities are references to any services or facilities whatever including, in particular—

(a) the provision of credit or of banking or insurance services and the provision of facilities incidental to the provision of such services;

(b) the purchase or sale of foreign currency;

(c) the supply of electricity;

(d) the provision of a place, other than on a highway, for the parking of a motor vehicle;

(e) the making of arrangements for a person to put or keep a caravan on any land other than arrangements by virtue of which that person may occupy the caravan as his only or main residence.

(2) References in this Part to services shall not include references to services provided to an employer under a contract of employment.

(3) References in this Part to services or facilities shall not include references to services or facilities which are provided by an authorised person or appointed representative in the course of the carrying on of an investment business.

(4) In relation to a service consisting in the purchase or sale of foreign currency, references in this Part to the method by which the price of the service is determined shall include references to the rate of exchange.

(5) In this section—

"appointed representative", "authorised person" and "investment
1986 c.60.   business" have the same meanings as in the Financial Services Act 1986;

"caravan" has the same meaning as in the Caravan Sites and Control of Development Act 1960;

PART III
1960 c.62.

"contract of employment" and "employer" have the same meanings as in the Employment Protection (Consolidation) Act 1978;

1978 c.44.

"credit" has the same meaning as in the Consumer Credit Act 1974.

1974 c.39.

23.—(1) Subject to subsection (2) below, references in this Part to accommodation or facilities being available shall not include references to accommodation or facilities being available to be provided by means of the creation or disposal of an interest in land except where—

Application to provision of accommodation etc.

(a) the person who is to create or dispose of the interest will do so in the course of any business of his; and

(b) the interest to be created or disposed of is a relevant interest in a new dwelling and is to be created or disposed of for the purpose of enabling that dwelling to be occupied as a residence, or one of the residences, of the person acquiring the interest.

(2) Subsection (1) above shall not prevent the application of any provision of this Part in relation to—

(a) the supply of any goods as part of the same transaction as any creation or disposal of an interest in land; or

(b) the provision of any services or facilities for the purposes of, or in connection with, any transaction for the creation or disposal of such an interest.

(3) In this section—

"new dwelling" means any building or part of a building in Great Britain which—

(a) has been constructed or adapted to be occupied as a residence; and

(b) has not previously been so occupied or has been so occupied only with other premises or as more than one residence,

and includes any yard, garden, out-houses or appurtenances which belong to that building or part or are to be enjoyed with it;

"relevant interest"—

(a) in relation to a new dwelling in England and Wales, means the freehold estate in the dwelling or a leasehold interest in the dwelling for a term of years absolute of more than twenty-one years, not being a term of which twenty-one years or less remains unexpired;

(b) in relation to a new dwelling in Scotland, means the *dominium utile* of the land comprising the dwelling, or a leasehold interest in the dwelling where twenty-one years or more remains unexpired.

24.—(1) In any proceedings against a person for an offence under subsection (1) or (2) of section 20 above in respect of any indication it shall be a defence for that person to show that his acts or omissions were authorised for the purposes of this subsection by regulations made under section 26 below.

Defences.

PART III   (2) In proceedings against a person for an offence under subsection (1) or (2) of section 20 above in respect of an indication published in a book, newspaper, magazine, film or radio or television broadcast or in a programme included in a cable programme service, it shall be a defence for that person to show that the indication was not contained in an advertisement.

(3) In proceedings against a person for an offence under subsection (1) or (2) of section 20 above in respect of an indication published in an advertisement it shall be a defence for that person to show that—

    (a) he is a person who carries on a business of publishing or arranging for the publication of advertisements;

    (b) he received the advertisement for publication in the ordinary course of that business; and

    (c) at the time of publication he did not know and had no grounds for suspecting that the publication would involve the commission of the offence.

(4) In any proceedings against a person for an offence under subsection (1) of section 20 above in respect of any indication, it shall be a defence for that person to show that—

    (a) the indication did not relate to the availability from him of any goods, services, accommodation or facilities;

    (b) a price had been recommended to every person from whom the goods, services, accommodation or facilities were indicated as being available;

    (c) the indication related to that price and was misleading as to that price only by reason of a failure by any person to follow the recommendation; and

    (d) it was reasonable for the person who gave the indication to assume that the recommendation was for the most part being followed.

(5) The provisions of this section are without prejudice to the provisions of section 39 below.

(6) In this section—

"advertisement" includes a catalogue, a circular and a price list;

1984 c.46.   "cable programme service" has the same meaning as in the Cable and Broadcasting Act 1984.

Code of practice.   **25.**—(1) The Secretary of State may, after consulting the Director General of Fair Trading and such other persons as the Secretary of State considers it appropriate to consult, by order approve any code of practice issued (whether by the Secretary of State or another person) for the purpose of—

    (a) giving practical guidance with respect to any of the requirements of section 20 above; and

    (b) promoting what appear to the Secretary of State to be desirable practices as to the circumstances and manner in which any person gives an indication as to the price at which any goods, services, accommodation or facilities are available or indicates any other matter in respect of which any such indication may be misleading.

(2) A contravention of a code of practice approved under this section shall not of itself give rise to any criminal or civil liability, but in any proceedings against any person for an offence under section 20(1) or (2) above—

   (a) any contravention by that person of such a code may be relied on in relation to any matter for the purpose of establishing that that person committed the offence or of negativing any defence; and

   (b) compliance by that person with such a code may be relied on in relation to any matter for the purpose of showing that the commission of the offence by that person has not been established or that that person has a defence.

(3) Where the Secretary of State approves a code of practice under this section he may, after such consultation as is mentioned in subsection (1) above, at any time by order—

   (a) approve any modification of the code; or

   (b) withdraw his approval;

and references in subsection (2) above to a code of practice approved under this section shall be construed accordingly.

(4) The power to make an order under this section shall be exercisable by statutory instrument subject to annulment in pursuance of a resolution of either House of Parliament.

26.—(1) The Secretary of State may, after consulting the Director General of Fair Trading and such other persons as the Secretary of State considers it appropriate to consult, by regulations make provision— Power to make regulations.

   (a) for the purpose of regulating the circumstances and manner in which any person—

   (i) gives any indication as to the price at which any goods, services, accommodation or facilities will be or are available or have been supplied or provided; or

   (ii) indicates any other matter in respect of which any such indication may be misleading;

   (b) for the purpose of facilitating the enforcement of the provisions of section 20 above or of any regulations made under this section.

(2) The Secretary of State shall not make regulations by virtue of subsection (1)(a) above except in relation to—

   (a) indications given by persons in the course of business; and

   (b) such indications given otherwise than in the course of business as—

   (i) are given by or on behalf of persons by whom accommodation is provided to others by means of leases or licences; and

   (ii) relate to goods, services or facilities supplied or provided to those others in connection with the provision of the accommodation.

(3) Without prejudice to the generality of subsection (1) above, regulations under this section may—

   (a) prohibit an indication as to a price from referring to such matters as may be prescribed by the regulations;

    (b) require an indication as to a price or other matter to be accompanied or supplemented by such explanation or such additional information as may be prescribed by the regulations;

    (c) require information or explanations with respect to a price or other matter to be given to an officer of an enforcement authority and to authorise such an officer to require such information or explanations to be given;

    (d) require any information or explanation provided for the purposes of any regulations made by virtue of paragraph (b) or (c) above to be accurate;

    (e) prohibit the inclusion in indications as to a price or other matter of statements that the indications are not to be relied upon;

    (f) provide that expressions used in any indication as to a price or other matter shall be construed in a particular way for the purposes of this Part;

    (g) provide that a contravention of any provision of the regulations shall constitute a criminal offence punishable—

        (i) on conviction on indictment, by a fine;

        (ii) on summary conviction, by a fine not exceeding the statutory maximum;

    (h) apply any provision of this Act which relates to a criminal offence to an offence created by virtue of paragraph (g) above.

(4) The power to make regulations under this section shall be exercisable by statutory instrument subject to annulment in pursuance of a resolution of either House of Parliament and shall include power—

    (a) to make different provision for different cases; and

    (b) to make such supplemental, consequential and transitional provision as the Secretary of State considers appropriate.

(5) In this section "lease" includes a sub-lease and an agreement for a lease and a statutory tenancy (within the meaning of the Landlord and Tenant Act 1985 or the Rent (Scotland) Act 1984).

1985 c. 70.
1984 c. 58.

PART IV

ENFORCEMENT OF PARTS II AND III

Enforcement.

27.—(1) Subject to the following provisions of this section—

    (a) it shall be the duty of every weights and measures authority in Great Britain to enforce within their area the safety provisions and the provisions made by or under Part III of this Act; and

    (b) it shall be the duty of every district council in Northern Ireland to enforce within their area the safety provisions.

(2) The Secretary of State may by regulations—

    (a) wholly or partly transfer any duty imposed by subsection (1) above on a weights and measures authority or a district council in Northern Ireland to such other person who has agreed to the transfer as is specified in the regulations;

    (b) relieve such an authority or council of any such duty so far as it is exercisable in relation to such goods as may be described in the regulations.

(3) The power to make regulations under subsection (2) above shall be exercisable by statutory instrument subject to annulment in pursuance of a resolution of either House of Parliament and shall include power—

    (a) to make different provision for different cases; and

    (b) to make such supplemental, consequential and transitional provision as the Secretary of State considers appropriate.

(4) Nothing in this section shall authorise any weights and measures authority, or any person on whom functions are conferred by regulations under subsection (2) above, to bring proceedings in Scotland for an offence.

28.—(1) An enforcement authority shall have power, for the purpose of ascertaining whether any safety provision or any provision made by or under Part III of this Act has been contravened in relation to any goods, services, accommodation or facilities— Test purchases.

    (a) to make, or to authorise an officer of the authority to make, any purchase of any goods; or

    (b) to secure, or to authorise an officer of the authority to secure, the provision of any services, accommodation or facilities.

(2) Where—

    (a) any goods purchased under this section by or on behalf of an enforcement authority are submitted to a test; and

    (b) the test leads to—

        (i) the bringing of proceedings for an offence in respect of a contravention in relation to the goods of any safety provision or of any provision made by or under Part III of this Act or for the forfeiture of the goods under section 16 or 17 above; or

        (ii) the serving of a suspension notice in respect of any goods; and

    (c) the authority is requested to do so and it is practicable for the authority to comply with the request,

the authority shall allow the person from whom the goods were purchased or any person who is a party to the proceedings or has an interest in any goods to which the notice relates to have the goods tested.

(3) The Secretary of State may by regulations provide that any test of goods purchased under this section by or on behalf of an enforcement authority shall—

    (a) be carried out at the expense of the authority in a manner and by a person prescribed by or determined under the regulations; or

    (b) be carried out either as mentioned in paragraph (a) above or by the authority in a manner prescribed by the regulations.

(4) The power to make regulations under subsection (3) above shall be exercisable by statutory instrument subject to annulment in pursuance of a resolution of either House of Parliament and shall include power—

    (a) to make different provision for different cases; and

(b) to make such supplemental, consequential and transitional provision as the Secretary of State considers appropriate.

(5) Nothing in this section shall authorise the acquisition by or on behalf of an enforcement authority of any interest in land.

Powers of search etc.

29.—(1) Subject to the following provisions of this Part, a duly authorised officer of an enforcement authority may at any reasonable hour and on production, if required, of his credentials exercise any of the powers conferred by the following provisions of this section.

(2) The officer may, for the purpose of ascertaining whether there has been any contravention of any safety provision or of any provision made by or under Part III of this Act, inspect any goods and enter any premises other than premises occupied only as a person's residence.

(3) The officer may, for the purpose of ascertaining whether there has been any contravention of any safety provision, examine any procedure (including any arrangements for carrying out a test) connected with the production of any goods.

(4) If the officer has reasonable grounds for suspecting that any goods are manufactured or imported goods which have not been supplied in the United Kingdom since they were manufactured or imported he may—

(a) for the purpose of ascertaining whether there has been any contravention of any safety provision in relation to the goods, require any person carrying on a business, or employed in connection with a business, to produce any records relating to the business;

(b) for the purpose of ascertaining (by testing or otherwise) whether there has been any such contravention, seize and detain the goods;

(c) take copies of, or of any entry in, any records produced by virtue of paragraph (a) above.

(5) If the officer has reasonable grounds for suspecting that there has been a contravention in relation to any goods of any safety provision or of any provision made by or under Part III of this Act, he may—

(a) for the purpose of ascertaining whether there has been any such contravention, require any person carrying on a business, or employed in connection with a business, to produce any records relating to the business;

(b) for the purpose of ascertaining (by testing or otherwise) whether there has been any such contravention, seize and detain the goods;

(c) take copies of, or of any entry in, any records produced by virtue of paragraph (a) above.

(6) The officer may seize and detain—

(a) any goods or records which he has reasonable grounds for believing may be required as evidence in proceedings for an offence in respect of a contravention of any safety provision or of any provision made by or under Part III of this Act;

(b) any goods which he has reasonable grounds for suspecting may be liable to be forfeited under section 16 or 17 above.

(7) If and to the extent that it is reasonably necessary to do so to prevent a contravention of any safety provision or of any provision made by or under Part III of this Act, the officer may, for the purpose of exercising his power under subsection (4), (5) or (6) above to seize any goods or records—

(a) require any person having authority to do so to open any container or to open any vending machine; and

(b) himself open or break open any such container or machine where a requirement made under paragraph (a) above in relation to the container or machine has not been complied with.

30.—(1) An officer seizing any goods or records under section 29 above shall inform the following persons that the goods or records have been so seized, that is to say—

(a) the person from whom they are seized; and

(b) in the case of imported goods seized on any premises under the control of the Commissioners of Customs and Excise, the importer of those goods (within the meaning of the Customs and Excise Management Act 1979).

(2) If a justice of the peace—

(a) is satisfied by any written information on oath that there are reasonable grounds for believing either—

(i) that any goods or records which any officer has power to inspect under section 29 above are on any premises and that their inspection is likely to disclose evidence that there has been a contravention of any safety provision or of any provision made by or under Part III of this Act; or

(ii) that such a contravention has taken place, is taking place or is about to take place on any premises; and

(b) is also satisfied by any such information either—

(i) that admission to the premises has been or is likely to be refused and that notice of intention to apply for a warrant under this subsection has been given to the occupier; or

(ii) that an application for admission, or the giving of such a notice, would defeat the object of the entry or that the premises are unoccupied or that the occupier is temporarily absent and it might defeat the object of the entry to await his return,

the justice may by warrant under his hand, which shall continue in force for a period of one month, authorise any officer of an enforcement authority to enter the premises, if need be by force.

(3) An officer entering any premises by virtue of section 29 above or a warrant under subsection (2) above may take with him such other persons and such equipment as may appear to him necessary.

(4) On leaving any premises which a person is authorised to enter by a warrant under subsection (2) above, that person shall, if the premises are unoccupied or the occupier is temporarily absent, leave the premises as effectively secured against trespassers as he found them.

(5) If any person who is not an officer of an enforcement authority purports to act as such under section 29 above or this section he shall be guilty of an offence and liable on summary conviction to a fine not exceeding level 5 on the standard scale.

(6) Where any goods seized by an officer under section 29 above are submitted to a test, the officer shall inform the persons mentioned in subsection (1) above of the result of the test and, if—

    (a) proceedings are brought for an offence in respect of a contravention in relation to the goods of any safety provision or of any provision made by or under Part III of this Act or for the forfeiture of the goods under section 16 or 17 above, or a suspension notice is served in respect of any goods; and

    (b) the officer is requested to do so and it is practicable to comply with the request,

the officer shall allow any person who is a party to the proceedings or, as the case may be, has an interest in the goods to which the notice relates to have the goods tested.

(7) The Secretary of State may by regulations provide that any test of goods seized under section 29 above by an officer of an enforcement authority shall—

    (a) be carried out at the expense of the authority in a manner and by a person prescribed by or determined under the regulations; or

    (b) be carried out either as mentioned in paragraph (a) above or by the authority in a manner prescribed by the regulations.

(8) The power to make regulations under subsection (7) above shall be exercisable by statutory instrument subject to annulment in pursuance of a resolution of either House of Parliament and shall include power—

    (a) to make different provision for different cases; and

    (b) to make such supplemental, consequential and transitional provision as the Secretary of State considers appropriate.

(9) In the application of this section to Scotland, the reference in subsection (2) above to a justice of the peace shall include a reference to a sheriff and the references to written information on oath shall be construed as references to evidence on oath.

(10) In the application of this section to Northern Ireland, the references in subsection (2) above to any information on oath shall be construed as references to any complaint on oath.

Power of customs officer to detain goods.

31.—(1) A customs officer may, for the purpose of facilitating the exercise by an enforcement authority or officer of such an authority of any functions conferred on the authority or officer by or under Part II of this Act, or by or under this Part in its application for the purposes of the safety provisions, seize any imported goods and detain them for not more than two working days.

(2) Anything seized and detained under this section shall be dealt with during the period of its detention in such manner as the Commissioners of Customs and Excise may direct.

(3) In subsection (1) above the reference to two working days is a reference to a period of forty-eight hours calculated from the time when the goods in question are seized but disregarding so much of any period as falls on a Saturday or Sunday or on Christmas Day, Good Friday or a day which is a bank holiday under the Banking and Financial Dealings Act 1971 in the part of the United Kingdom where the goods are seized.

(4) In this section and section 32 below "customs officer" means any officer within the meaning of the Customs and Excise Management Act 1979.

32.—(1) Any person who—

   (a) intentionally obstructs any officer of an enforcement authority who is acting in pursuance of any provision of this Part or any customs officer who is so acting; or

   (b) intentionally fails to comply with any requirement made of him by any officer of an enforcement authority under any provision of this Part; or

   (c) without reasonable cause fails to give any officer of an enforcement authority who is so acting any other assistance or information which the officer may reasonably require of him for the purposes of the exercise of the officer's functions under any provision of this Part,

shall be guilty of an offence and liable on summary conviction to a fine not exceeding level 5 on the standard scale.

(2) A person shall be guilty of an offence if, in giving any information which is required of him by virtue of subsection (1)(c) above—

   (a) he makes any statement which he knows is false in a material particular; or

   (b) he recklessly makes a statement which is false in a material particular.

(3) A person guilty of an offence under subsection (2) above shall be liable—

   (a) on conviction on indictment, to a fine;

   (b) on summary conviction, to a fine not exceeding the statutory maximum.

33.—(1) Any person having an interest in any goods which are for the time being detained under any provision of this Part by an enforcement authority or by an officer of such an authority may apply for an order requiring the goods to be released to him or to another person.

(2) An application under this section may be made—

   (a) to any magistrates' court in which proceedings have been brought in England and Wales or Northern Ireland—

      (i) for an offence in respect of a contravention in relation to the goods of any safety provision or of any provision made by or under Part III of this Act; or

      (ii) for the forfeiture of the goods under section 16 above;

   (b) where no such proceedings have been so brought, by way of complaint to a magistrates' court; or

(c)   in Scotland, by summary application to the sheriff.

(3) On an application under this section to a magistrates' court or to the sheriff, an order requiring goods to be released shall be made only if the court or sheriff is satisfied—

(a)   that proceedings—

(i)   for an offence in respect of a contravention in relation to the goods of any safety provision or of any provision made by or under Part III of this Act; or

(ii) for the forfeiture of the goods under section 16 or 17 above,

have not been brought or, having been brought, have been concluded without the goods being forfeited; and

(b)   where no such proceedings have been brought, that more than six months have elapsed since the goods were seized.

(4) Any person aggrieved by an order made under this section by a magistrates' court in England and Wales or Northern Ireland, or by a decision of such a court not to make such an order, may appeal against that order or decision—

(a)   in England and Wales, to the Crown Court;

(b)   in Northern Ireland, to the county court;

and an order so made may contain such provision as appears to the court to be appropriate for delaying the coming into force of the order pending the making and determination of any appeal (including any application under section 111 of the Magistrates' Courts Act 1980 or Article 146 of the Magistrates' Courts (Northern Ireland) Order 1981 (statement of case)).

1980 c. 43.
S.I. 1981/1675
(N.I. 26).

Compensation for
seizure and
detention.

34.—(1) Where an officer of an enforcement authority exercises any power under section 29 above to seize and detain goods, the enforcement authority shall be liable to pay compensation to any person having an interest in the goods in respect of any loss or damage caused by reason of the exercise of the power if—

(a)   there has been no contravention in relation to the goods of any safety provision or of any provision made by or under Part III of this Act; and

(b)   the exercise of the power is not attributable to any neglect or default by that person.

(2) Any disputed question as to the right to or the amount of any compensation payable under this section shall be determined by arbitration or, in Scotland, by a single arbiter appointed, failing agreement between the parties, by the sheriff.

Recovery of
expenses of
enforcement.

35.—(1) This section shall apply where a court—

(a)   convicts a person of an offence in respect of a contravention in relation to any goods of any safety provision or of any provision made by or under Part III of this Act; or

(b) makes an order under section 16 or 17 above for the forfeiture of any goods.

(2) The court may (in addition to any other order it may make as to costs or expenses) order the person convicted or, as the case may be, any person having an interest in the goods to reimburse an enforcement authority for any expenditure which has been or may be incurred by that authority—

(a) in connection with any seizure or detention of the goods by or on behalf of the authority; or

(b) in connection with any compliance by the authority with directions given by the court for the purposes of any order for the forfeiture of the goods.

PART V

MISCELLANEOUS AND SUPPLEMENTAL

36. Part I of the Health and Safety at Work etc. Act 1974 (which includes provision with respect to the safety of certain articles and substances) shall have effect with the amendments specified in Schedule 3 to this Act; and, accordingly, the general purposes of that Part of that Act shall include the purpose of protecting persons from the risks protection from which would not be afforded by virtue of that Part but for those amendments.

37.—(1) If they think it appropriate to do so for the purpose of facilitating the exercise by any person to whom subsection (2) below applies of any functions conferred on that person by or under Part II of this Act, or by or under Part IV of this Act in its application for the purposes of the safety provisions, the Commissioners of Customs and Excise may authorise the disclosure to that person of any information obtained for the purposes of the exercise by the Commissioners of their functions in relation to imported goods.

(2) This subsection applies to an enforcement authority and to any officer of an enforcement authority.

(3) A disclosure of information made to any person under subsection (1) above shall be made in such manner as may be directed by the Commissioners of Customs and Excise and may be made through such persons acting on behalf of that person as may be so directed.

(4) Information may be disclosed to a person under subsection (1) above whether or not the disclosure of the information has been requested by or on behalf of that person.

38.—(1) Subject to the following provisions of this section, a person shall be guilty of an offence if he discloses any information—

(a) which was obtained by him in consequence of its being given to any person in compliance with any requirement imposed by safety regulations or regulations under section 26 above;

(b) which consists in a secret manufacturing process or a trade secret and was obtained by him in consequence of the inclusion of the information—

        (i) in written or oral representations made for the purposes of Part I or II of Schedule 2 to this Act; or

        (ii) in a statement of a witness in connection with any such oral representations;

(c) which was obtained by him in consequence of the exercise by the Secretary of State of the power conferred by section 18 above;

(d) which was obtained by him in consequence of the exercise by any person of any power conferred by Part IV of this Act; or

(e) which was disclosed to or through him under section 37 above.

(2) Subsection (1) above shall not apply to a disclosure of information if the information is publicised information or the disclosure is made—

(a) for the purpose of facilitating the exercise of a relevant person's functions under this Act or any enactment or subordinate legislation mentioned in subsection (3) below;

(b) for the purposes of compliance with a Community obligation; or

(c) in connection with the investigation of any criminal offence or for the purposes of any civil or criminal proceedings.

(3) The enactments and subordinate legislation referred to in subsection (2)(a) above are—

1968 c. 29.   (a) the Trade Descriptions Act 1968;

1973 c. 41.   (b) Parts II and III and section 125 of the Fair Trading Act 1973;

1974 c. 37.
S.I. 1978/1039
(N.I.9).
    (c) the relevant statutory provisions within the meaning of Part I of the Health and Safety at Work etc. Act 1974 or within the meaning of the Health and Safety at Work (Northern Ireland) Order 1978;

1974 c. 39.   (d) the Consumer Credit Act 1974;

1976 c. 34.   (e) the Restrictive Trade Practices Act 1976;

1976 c. 53.   (f) the Resale Prices Act 1976;

1979 c. 38.   (g) the Estate Agents Act 1979;

1980 c. 21.   (h) the Competition Act 1980;

1984 c. 12.   (i) the Telecommunications Act 1984;

1986 c. 31.   (j) the Airports Act 1986;

1986 c. 44.   (k) the Gas Act 1986;

(l) any subordinate legislation made (whether before or after the passing of this Act) for the purpose of securing compliance with the Directive of the Council of the European Communities, dated 10th September 1984 (No. 84/450/EEC) on the approximation of the laws, regulations and administrative provisions of the member States concerning misleading advertising.

(4) In subsection (2)(a) above the reference to a person's functions shall include a reference to any function of making, amending or revoking any regulations or order.

(5) A person guilty of an offence under this section shall be liable—

(a) on summary conviction, to a fine not exceeding the statutory maximum;

(b) on conviction on indictment, to imprisonment for a term not exceeding two years or to a fine or to both.

(6) In this section—

"publicised information" means any information which has been disclosed in any civil or criminal proceedings or is or has been required to be contained in a warning published in pursuance of a notice to warn; and

"relevant person" means any of the following, that is to say—

(a) a Minister of the Crown, Government department or Northern Ireland department;

(b) the Monopolies and Mergers Commission, the Director General of Fair Trading, the Director General of Telecommunications or the Director General of Gas Supply;

(c) the Civil Aviation Authority;

(d) any weights and measures authority, any district council in Northern Ireland or any person on whom functions are conferred by regulations under section 27(2) above;

(e) any person who is an enforcing authority for the purposes of Part I of the Health and Safety at Work etc. Act 1974 or for the purposes of Part II of the Health and Safety at Work (Northern Ireland) Order 1978.

1974 c. 37.
S.I. 1978/1039
(N.I.9).

39.—(1) Subject to the following provisions of this section, in proceedings against any person for an offence to which this section applies it shall be a defence for that person to show that he took all reasonable steps and exercised all due diligence to avoid committing the offence.

Defence of due diligence.

(2) Where in any proceedings against any person for such an offence the defence provided by subsection (1) above involves an allegation that the commission of the offence was due—

(a) to the act or default of another; or

(b) to reliance on information given by another,

that person shall not, without the leave of the court, be entitled to rely on the defence unless, not less than seven clear days before the hearing of the proceedings, he has served a notice under subsection (3) below on the person bringing the proceedings.

(3) A notice under this subsection shall give such information identifying or assisting in the identification of the person who committed the act or default or gave the information as is in the possession of the person serving the notice at the time he serves it.

(4) It is hereby declared that a person shall not be entitled to rely on the defence provided by subsection (1) above by reason of his reliance on information supplied by another, unless he shows that it was reasonable in all the circumstances for him to have relied on the information, having regard in particular—

(a) to the steps which he took, and those which might reasonably have been taken, for the purpose of verifying the information; and

(b) to whether he had any reason to disbelieve the information.

(5) This section shall apply to an offence under section 10, 12(1), (2) or (3), 13(4), 14(6) or 20(1) above.

40.—(1) Where the commission by any person of an offence to which section 39 above applies is due to an act or default committed by some other person in the course of any business of his, the other person shall be guilty of the offence and may be proceeded against and punished by virtue of this subsection whether or not proceedings are taken against the first-mentioned person.

(2) Where a body corporate is guilty of an offence under this Act (including where it is so guilty by virtue of subsection (1) above) in respect of any act or default which is shown to have been committed with the consent or connivance of, or to be attributable to any neglect on the part of, any director, manager, secretary or other similar officer of the body corporate or any person who was purporting to act in any such capacity he, as well as the body corporate, shall be guilty of that offence and shall be liable to be proceeded against and punished accordingly.

(3) Where the affairs of a body corporate are managed by its members, subsection (2) above shall apply in relation to the acts and defaults of a member in connection with his functions of management as if he were a director of the body corporate.

41.—(1) An obligation imposed by safety regulations shall be a duty owed to any person who may be affected by a contravention of the obligation and, subject to any provision to the contrary in the regulations and to the defences and other incidents applying to actions for breach of statutory duty, a contravention of any such obligation shall be actionable accordingly.

(2) This Act shall not be construed as conferring any other right of action in civil proceedings, apart from the right conferred by virtue of Part I of this Act, in respect of any loss or damage suffered in consequence of a contravention of a safety provision or of a provision made by or under Part III of this Act.

(3) Subject to any provision to the contrary in the agreement itself, an agreement shall not be void or unenforceable by reason only of a contravention of a safety provision or of a provision made by or under Part III of this Act.

(4) Liability by virtue of subsection (1) above shall not be limited or excluded by any contract term, by any notice or (subject to the power contained in subsection (1) above to limit or exclude it in safety regulations) by any other provision.

(5) Nothing in subsection (1) above shall prejudice the operation of section 12 of the Nuclear Installations Act 1965 (rights to compensation for certain breaches of duties confined to rights under that Act).

(6) In this section "damage" includes personal injury and death.

42.—(1) It shall be the duty of the Secretary of State at least once in every five years to lay before each House of Parliament a report on the exercise during the period to which the report relates of the functions which under Part II of this Act, or under Part IV of this Act in its application for the purposes of the safety provisions, are exercisable by the Secretary of State, weights and measures authorities, district councils in Northern Ireland and persons on whom functions are conferred by regulations made under section 27(2) above.

(2) The Secretary of State may from time to time prepare and lay before each House of Parliament such other reports on the exercise of those functions as he considers appropriate.

(3) Every weights and measures authority, every district council in Northern Ireland and every person on whom functions are conferred by regulations under subsection (2) of section 27 above shall, whenever the Secretary of State so directs, make a report to the Secretary of State on the exercise of the functions exercisable by that authority or council under that section or by that person by virtue of any such regulations.

(4) A report under subsection (3) above shall be in such form and shall contain such particulars as are specified in the direction of the Secretary of State.

(5) The first report under subsection (1) above shall be laid before each House of Parliament not more than five years after the laying of the last report under section 8(2) of the Consumer Safety Act 1978.

1978 c. 38.

43.—(1) There shall be paid out of money provided by Parliament—

Financial provisions.

(a) any expenses incurred or compensation payable by a Minister of the Crown or Government department in consequence of any provision of this Act; and

(b) any increase attributable to this Act in the sums payable out of money so provided under any other Act.

(2) Any sums received by a Minister of the Crown or Government department by virtue of this Act shall be paid into the Consolidated Fund.

44.—(1) Any document required or authorised by virtue of this Act to be served on a person may be so served—

Service of documents etc.

(a) by delivering it to him or by leaving it at his proper address or by sending it by post to him at that address; or

(b) if the person is a body corporate, by serving it in accordance with paragraph (a) above on the secretary or clerk of that body; or

(c) if the person is a partnership, by serving it in accordance with that paragraph on a partner or on a person having control or management of the partnership business.

(2) For the purposes of subsection (1) above, and for the purposes of section 7 of the Interpretation Act 1978 (which relates to the service of documents by post) in its application to that subsection, the proper address of any person on whom a document is to be served by virtue of this Act shall be his last known address except that—

1978 c. 30.

(a) in the case of service on a body corporate or its secretary or clerk, it shall be the address of the registered or principal office of the body corporate;

(b) in the case of service on a partnership or a partner or a person having the control or management of a partnership business, it shall be the principal office of the partnership;

and for the purposes of this subsection the principal office of a company registered outside the United Kingdom or of a partnership carrying on business outside the United Kingdom is its principal office within the United Kingdom.

(3) The Secretary of State may by regulations make provision for the manner in which any information is to be given to any person under any provision of Part IV of this Act.

(4) Without prejudice to the generality of subsection (3) above regulations made by the Secretary of State may prescribe the person, or manner of determining the person, who is to be treated for the purposes of section 28(2) or 30 above as the person from whom any goods were purchased or seized where the goods were purchased or seized from a vending machine.

(5) The power to make regulations under subsection (3) or (4) above shall be exercisable by statutory instrument subject to annulment in pursuance of a resolution of either House of Parliament and shall include power—

(a) to make different provision for different cases; and

(b) to make such supplemental, consequential and transitional provision as the Secretary of State considers appropriate.

Interpretation.

45.—(1) In this Act, except in so far as the context otherwise requires—

"aircraft" includes gliders, balloons and hovercraft;

"business" includes a trade or profession and the activities of a professional or trade association or of a local authority or other public authority;

"conditional sale agreement", "credit—sale agreement" and "hire-purchase agreement" have the same meanings as in the Consumer Credit Act 1974 but as if in the definitions in that Act "goods" had the same meaning as in this Act;

1974 c. 39.

"contravention" includes a failure to comply and cognate expressions shall be construed accordingly;

"enforcement authority" means the Secretary of State, any other Minister of the Crown in charge of a Government department, any such department and any authority, council or other person on whom functions under this Act are conferred by or under section 27 above;

1986 c. 44.

"gas" has the same meaning as in Part I of the Gas Act 1986;

"goods" includes substances, growing crops and things comprised in land by virtue of being attached to it and any ship, aircraft or vehicle;

"information" includes accounts, estimates and returns;

"magistrates' court", in relation to Northern Ireland, means a court of summary jurisdiction;

1938 c. 22.

"mark" and "trade mark" have the same meanings as in the Trade Marks Act 1938;

"modifications" includes additions, alterations and omissions, and cognate expressions shall be construed accordingly;

1972 c. 20.

"motor vehicle" has the same meaning as in the Road Traffic Act 1972;

"notice" means a notice in writing;

"notice to warn" means a notice under section 13(1)(b) above;

"officer", in relation to an enforcement authority, means a person authorised in writing to assist the authority in carrying out its functions under or for the purposes of the enforcement of any of the safety provisions or of any of the provisions made by or under Part III of this Act;

"personal injury" includes any disease and any other impairment of a person's physical or mental condition;

"premises" includes any place and any ship, aircraft or vehicle;

"prohibition notice" means a notice under section 13(1)(a) above;

"records" includes any books or documents and any records in non-documentary form;

"safety provision" means the general safety requirement in section 10 above or any provision of safety regulations, a prohibition notice or a suspension notice;

"safety regulations" means regulations under section 11 above;

"ship" includes any boat and any other description of vessel used in navigation;

"subordinate legislation" has the same meaning as in the Interpretation Act 1978;

1978 c. 30.

"substance" means any natural or artificial substance, whether in solid, liquid or gaseous form or in the form of a vapour, and includes substances that are comprised in or mixed with other goods;

"supply" and cognate expressions shall be construed in accordance with section 46 below;

"suspension notice" means a notice under section 14 above.

(2) Except in so far as the context otherwise requires, references in this Act to a contravention of a safety provision shall, in relation to any goods, include references to anything which would constitute such a contravention if the goods were supplied to any person.

(3) References in this Act to any goods in relation to which any safety provision has been or may have been contravened shall include references to any goods which it is not reasonably practicable to separate from any such goods.

(4) Section 68(2) of the Trade Marks Act 1938 (construction of references to use of a mark) shall apply for the purposes of this Act as it applies for the purposes of that Act.

1938 c. 22.

(5) In Scotland, any reference in this Act to things comprised in land by virtue of being attached to it is a reference to moveables which have become heritable by accession to heritable property.

46.—(1) Subject to the following provisions of this section, references in this Act to supplying goods shall be construed as references to doing any of the following, whether as principal or agent, that is to say—

Meaning of "supply".

(a) selling, hiring out or lending the goods;

(b) entering into a hire-purchase agreement to furnish the goods;

(c) the performance of any contract for work and materials to furnish the goods;

(d) providing the goods in exchange for any consideration (including trading stamps) other than money;

(e) providing the goods in or in connection with the performance of any statutory function; or

(f) giving the goods as a prize or otherwise making a gift of the goods;

and, in relation to gas or water, those references shall be construed as including references to providing the service by which the gas or water is made available for use.

(2) For the purposes of any reference in this Act to supplying goods, where a person ("the ostensible supplier") supplies goods to another person ("the customer") under a hire-purchase agreement, conditional sale agreement or credit-sale agreement or under an agreement for the hiring of goods (other than a hire-purchase agreement) and the ostensible supplier—

(a) carries on the business of financing the provision of goods for others by means of such agreements; and

(b) in the course of that business acquired his interest in the goods supplied to the customer as a means of financing the provision of them for the customer by a further person ("the effective supplier"),

the effective supplier and not the ostensible supplier shall be treated as supplying the goods to the customer.

(3) Subject to subsection (4) below, the performance of any contract by the erection of any building or structure on any land or by the carrying out of any other building works shall be treated for the purposes of this Act as a supply of goods in so far as, but only in so far as, it involves the provision of any goods to any person by means of their incorporation into the building, structure or works.

(4) Except for the purposes of, and in relation to, notices to warn or any provision made by or under Part III of this Act, references in this Act to supplying goods shall not include references to supplying goods comprised in land where the supply is effected by the creation or disposal of an interest in the land.

(5) Except in Part I of this Act references in this Act to a person's supplying goods shall be confined to references to that person's supplying goods in the course of a business of his, but for the purposes of this subsection it shall be immaterial whether the business is a business of dealing in the goods.

(6) For the purposes of subsection (5) above goods shall not be treated as supplied in the course of a business if they are supplied, in pursuance of an obligation arising under or in connection with the insurance of the goods, to the person with whom they were insured.

(7) Except for the purposes of, and in relation to, prohibition notices or suspension notices, references in Parts II to IV of this Act to supplying goods shall not include—

(a) references to supplying goods where the person supplied carries on a business of buying goods of the same description as those goods and repairing or reconditioning them;

(b) references to supplying goods by a sale of articles as scrap (that is to say, for the value of materials included in the articles rather than for the value of the articles themselves).

(8) Where any goods have at any time been supplied by being hired out or lent to any person, neither a continuation or renewal of the hire or loan (whether on the same or different terms) nor any transaction for the transfer after that time of any interest in the goods to the person to whom they were hired or lent shall be treated for the purposes of this Act as a further supply of the goods to that person.

(9) A ship, aircraft or motor vehicle shall not be treated for the purposes of this Act as supplied to any person by reason only that services consisting in the carriage of goods or passengers in that ship, aircraft or vehicle, or in its use for any other purpose, are provided to that person in pursuance of an agreement relating to the use of the ship, aircraft or vehicle for a particular period or for particular voyages, flights or journeys.

47.—(1) Nothing in this Act shall be taken as requiring any person to produce any records if he would be entitled to refuse to produce those records in any proceedings in any court on the grounds that they are the subject of legal professional privilege or, in Scotland, that they contain a confidential communication made by or to an advocate or solicitor in that capacity, or as authorising any person to take possession of any records which are in the possession of a person who would be so entitled. *Savings for certain privileges.*

(2) Nothing in this Act shall be construed as requiring a person to answer any question or give any information if to do so would incriminate that person or that person's spouse.

48.—(1) The enactments mentioned in Schedule 4 to this Act shall have effect subject to the amendments specified in that Schedule (being minor amendments and amendments consequential on the provisions of this Act). *Minor and consequential amendments and repeals.*

(2) The following Acts shall cease to have effect, that is to say—

    (a) the Trade Descriptions Act 1972; and   *1972 c.34.*

    (b) the Fabrics (Misdescription) Act 1913.   *1913 c.17.*

(3) The enactments mentioned in Schedule 5 to this Act are hereby repealed to the extent specified in the third column of that Schedule.

49.—(1) This Act shall extend to Northern Ireland with the exception of— *Northern Ireland.*

    (a) the provisions of Parts I and III;

    (b) any provision amending or repealing an enactment which does not so extend; and

    (c) any other provision so far as it has effect for the purposes of, or in relation to, a provision falling within paragraph (a) or (b) above.

(2) Subject to any Order in Council made by virtue of subsection (1)(a) of section 3 of the Northern Ireland Constitution Act 1973, consumer safety shall not be a transferred matter for the purposes of that Act but shall for the purposes of subsection (2) of that section be treated as specified in Schedule 3 to that Act. *1973 c.36.*

(3) An Order in Council under paragraph 1(1)(b) of Schedule 1 to the Northern Ireland Act 1974 (exercise of legislative functions for Northern Ireland) which states that it is made only for purposes corresponding to any of the provisions of this Act mentioned in subsection (1)(a) to (c) above—

    (a) shall not be subject to paragraph 1(4) and (5) of that Schedule (affirmative resolution procedure and procedure in cases of urgency); but

    (b) shall be subject to annulment in pursuance of a resolution of either House of Parliament.

50.—(1) This Act may be cited as the Consumer Protection Act 1987.

(2) This Act shall come into force on such day as the Secretary of State may by order made by statutory instrument appoint, and different days may be so appointed for different provisions or for different purposes.

(3) The Secretary of State shall not make an order under subsection (2) above bringing into force the repeal of the Trade Descriptions Act 1972, a repeal of any provision of that Act or a repeal of that Act or of any provision of it for any purposes, unless a draft of the order has been laid before, and approved by a resolution of, each House of Parliament.

(4) An order under subsection (2) above bringing a provision into force may contain such transitional provision in connection with the coming into force of that provision as the Secretary of State considers appropriate.

(5) Without prejudice to the generality of the power conferred by subsection (4) above, the Secretary of State may by order provide for any regulations made under the Consumer Protection Act 1961 or the Consumer Protection Act (Northern Ireland) 1965 to have effect as if made under section 11 above and for any such regulations to have effect with such modifications as he considers appropriate for that purpose.

(6) The power of the Secretary of State by order to make such provision as is mentioned in subsection (5) above, shall, in so far as it is not exercised by an order under subsection (2) above, be exercisable by statutory instrument subject to annulment in pursuance of a resolution of either House of Parliament.

(7) Nothing in this Act or in any order under subsection (2) above shall make any person liable by virtue of Part I of this Act for any damage caused wholly or partly by a defect in a product which was supplied to any person by its producer before the coming into force of Part I of this Act.

(8) Expressions used in subsection (7) above and in Part I of this Act have the same meanings in that subsection as in that Part.

SCHEDULES

SCHEDULE 1

Limitation of Actions under Part I

Part I

England and Wales

1. After section 11 of the Limitation Act 1980 (actions in respect of personal injuries) there shall be inserted the following section—   1980 c. 58.

"Actions in respect of defective products.   11A.—(1) This section shall apply to an action for damages by virtue of any provision of Part I of the Consumer Protection Act 1987.

(2) None of the time limits given in the preceding provisions of this Act shall apply to an action to which this section applies.

(3) An action to which this section applies shall not be brought after the expiration of the period of ten years from the relevant time, within the meaning of section 4 of the said Act of 1987; and this subsection shall operate to extinguish a right of action and shall do so whether or not that right of action had accrued, or time under the following provisions of this Act had begun to run, at the end of the said period of ten years.

(4) Subject to subsection (5) below, an action to which this section applies in which the damages claimed by the plaintiff consist of or include damages in respect of personal injuries to the plaintiff or any other person or loss of or damage to any property, shall not be brought after the expiration of the period of three years from whichever is the later of—

(a) the date on which the cause of action accrued; and

(b) the date of knowledge of the injured person or, in the case of loss of or damage to property, the date of knowledge of the plaintiff or (if earlier) of any person in whom his cause of action was previously vested.

(5) If in a case where the damages claimed by the plaintiff consist of or include damages in respect of personal injuries to the plaintiff or any other person the injured person died before the expiration of the period mentioned in subsection (4) above, that subsection shall have effect as respects the cause of action surviving for the benefit of his estate by virtue of section 1 of the Law Reform (Miscellaneous   1934 c. 41. Provisions) Act 1934 as if for the reference to that period there were substituted a reference to the period of three years from whichever is the later of—

(a) the date of death; and

(b) the date of the personal representative's knowledge.

(6) For the purposes of this section 'personal representative' includes any person who is or has been a personal representative of the deceased, including an executor who has not proved the will (whether or not he has renounced probate) but not anyone appointed only as a special personal representative in relation to settled land; and regard shall be had to any knowledge acquired by any such person while a personal representative or previously.

(7) If there is more than one personal representative and their dates of knowledge are different, subsection (5)(b) above shall be read as referring to the earliest of those dates.

(8) Expressions used in this section or section 14 of this Act and in Part I of the Consumer Protection Act 1987 have the same meanings in this section or that section as in that Part; and section 1(1) of that Act (Part I to be construed as enacted for the purpose of complying with the product liability Directive) shall apply for the purpose of construing this section and the following provisions of this Act so far as they relate to an action by virtue of any provision of that Part as it applies for the purpose of construing that Part."

2. In section 12(1) of the said Act of 1980 (actions under the Fatal Accidents Act 1976), after the words "section 11" there shall be inserted the words "or 11A".

3. In section 14 of the said Act of 1980 (definition of date of knowledge), in subsection (1), at the beginning there shall be inserted the words "Subject to subsection (1A) below," and after that subsection there shall be inserted the following subsection—

"(1A) In section 11A of this Act and in section 12 of this Act so far as that section applies to an action by virtue of section 6(1)(a) of the Consumer Protection Act 1987 (death caused by defective product) references to a person's date of knowledge are references to the date on which he first had knowledge of the following facts—

(a) such facts about the damage caused by the defect as would lead a reasonable person who had suffered such damage to consider it sufficiently serious to justify his instituting proceedings for damages against a defendant who did not dispute liability and was able to satisfy a judgment; and

(b) that the damage was wholly or partly attributable to the facts and circumstances alleged to constitute the defect; and

(c) the identity of the defendant;

but, in determining the date on which a person first had such knowledge there shall be disregarded both the extent (if any) of that person's knowledge on any date of whether particular facts or circumstances would or would not, as a matter of law, constitute a defect and, in a case relating to loss of or damage to property, any knowledge which that person had on a date on which he had no right of action by virtue of Part I of that Act in respect of the loss or damage."

4. In section 28 of the said Act of 1980 (extension of limitation period in case of disability), after subsection (6) there shall be inserted the following subsection—

"(7) If the action is one to which section 11A of this Act applies or one by virtue of section 6(1)(a) of the Consumer Protection Act 1987 (death caused by defective product), subsection (1) above—

(a) shall not apply to the time limit prescribed by subsection (3) of the said section 11A or to that time limit as applied by virtue of section 12(1) of this Act; and

(b) in relation to any other time limit prescribed by this Act shall have effect as if for the words 'six years' there were substituted the words 'three years'."

5. In section 32 of the said Act of 1980 (postponement of limitation period in case of fraud, concealment or mistake)—

(a) in subsection (1), for the words "subsection (3)" there shall be substituted the words "subsections (3) and (4A)"; and

(b) after subsection (4) there shall be inserted the following subsection—

> "(4A) Subsection (1) above shall not apply in relation to the time limit prescribed by section 11A(3) of this Act or in relation to that time limit as applied by virtue of section 12(1) of this Act."

6. In section 33 of the said Act of 1980 (discretionary exclusion of time limit)—

(a) in subsection (1), after the words "section 11" there shall be inserted the words "or 11A";

(b) after the said subsection (1) there shall be inserted the following subsection—

> "(1A) The court shall not under this section disapply—
>
> > (a) subsection (3) of section 11A; or
> >
> > (b) where the damages claimed by the plaintiff are confined to damages for loss of or damage to any property, any other provision in its application to an action by virtue of Part I of the Consumer Protection Act 1987.";

(c) in subsections (2) and (4), after the words "section 11" there shall be inserted the words "or subsection (4) of section 11A";

(d) in subsection (3)(b), after the words "section 11" there shall be inserted the words ", by section 11A"; and

(e) in subsection (8), after the words "section 11" there shall be inserted the words "or 11A".

PART II

SCOTLAND

7. The Prescription and Limitation (Scotland) Act 1973 shall be amended as follows.

8. In section 7(2), after the words "not being an obligation" there shall be inserted the words "to which section 22A of this Act applies or an obligation".

9. In Part II, before section 17, there shall be inserted the following section—

"Part II not to extend to product liability.
    16A.—This Part of this Act does not apply to any action to which section 22B or 22C of this Act applies."

10. After section 22, there shall be inserted the following new Part—

"PART IIA

PRESCRIPTION OF OBLIGATIONS AND LIMITATION OF ACTIONS UNDER PART I OF THE CONSUMER PROTECTION ACT 1987

Prescription of Obligations

Ten years' prescription of obligations.
    22A.—(1) An obligation arising from liability under section 2 of the 1987 Act (to make reparation for damage caused wholly or partly by a defect in a product) shall be extinguished if a period of 10 years has expired from the relevant time, unless a relevant claim was made within that period and has not been finally disposed of, and no such obligation shall come into existence after the expiration of the said period.

(2) If, at the expiration of the period of 10 years mentioned in subsection (1) above, a relevant claim has been made but has not been finally disposed of, the obligation to which the claim relates shall be extinguished when the claim is finally disposed of.

(3) In this section—

(a) a decision disposing of the claim has been made against which no appeal is competent;

(b) an appeal against such a decision is competent with leave, and the time limit for leave has expired and no application has been made or leave has been refused;

(c) leave to appeal against such a decision is granted or is not required, and no appeal is made within the time limit for appeal; or

(d) the claim is abandoned;

a claim is finally disposed of when 'relevant claim' in relation to an obligation means a claim made by or on behalf of the creditor for implement or part implement of the obligation, being a claim made—

(a) in appropriate proceedings within the meaning of section 4(2) of this Act; or

1985 c. 66.

(b) by the presentation of, or the concurring in, a petition for sequestration or by the submission of a claim under section 22 or 48 of the Bankruptcy (Scotland) Act 1985; or

1986 c. 45.

(c) by the presentation of, or the concurring in, a petition for the winding up of a company or by the submission of a claim in a liquidation in accordance with the rules made under section 411 of the Insolvency Act 1986;

'relevant time' has the meaning given in section 4(2) of the 1987 Act.

(4) Where a relevant claim is made in an arbitration, and the nature of the claim has been stated in a preliminary notice (within the meaning of section 4(4) of this Act) relating to that arbitration, the date when the notice is served shall be taken for those purposes to be the date of the making of the claim.

Limitation of actions

3 year limitation of actions.

22B—(1) This section shall apply to an action to enforce an obligation arising from liability under section 2 of the 1987 Act (to make reparation for damage caused wholly or partly by a defect in a product), except where section 22C of this Act applies.

(2) Subject to subsection (4) below, an action to which this section applies shall not be competent unless it is commenced within the period of 3 years after the earliest date on which the person seeking to bring (or a person who could at an earlier date have brought) the action was aware, or on which, in the opinion of the court, it was reasonably practicable for him in all the circumstances to become aware, of all the facts mentioned in subsection (3) below.

(3) The facts referred to in subsection (2) above are—

(a) that there was a defect in a product;

(b) that the damage was caused or partly caused by the defect;

(c) that the damage was sufficiently serious to justify the pursuer (or other person referred to in subsection (2) above) in bringing an action to which this section applies on the assumption that the defender did not dispute liability and was able to satisfy a decree;

(d) that the defender was a person liable for the damage under the said section 2.

(4) In the computation of the period of 3 years mentioned in subsection (2) above, there shall be disregarded any period during which the person seeking to bring the action was under legal disability by reason of nonage or unsoundness of mind.

(5) The facts mentioned in subsection (3) above do not include knowledge of whether particular facts and circumstances would or would not, as a matter of law, result in liability for damage under the said section 2.

(6) Where a person would be entitled, but for this section, to bring an action for reparation other than one in which the damages claimed are confined to damages for loss of or damage to property, the court may, if it seems to it equitable to do so, allow him to bring the action notwithstanding this section.

Actions under the 1987 Act where death has resulted from personal injuries. 22C.—(1) This section shall apply to an action to enforce an obligation arising from liability under section 2 of the 1987 Act (to make reparation for damage caused wholly or partly by a defect in a product) where a person has died from personal injuries and the damages claimed include damages for those personal injuries or that death.

(2) Subject to subsection (4) below, an action to which this section applies shall not be competent unless it is commenced within the period of 3 years after the later of—

(a) the date of death of the injured person;

(b) the earliest date on which the person seeking to make (or a person who could at an earlier date have made) the claim was aware, or on which, in the opinion of the court, it was reasonably practicable for him in all the circumstances to become aware—

(i) that there was a defect in the product;

(ii) that the injuries of the deceased were caused (or partly caused) by the defect; and

(iii) that the defender was a person liable for the damage under the said section 2.

(3) Where the person seeking to make the claim is a relative of the deceased, there shall be disregarded in the computation of the period mentioned in subsection (2) above any period during which that relative was under legal disability by reason of nonage or unsoundness of mind.

(4) Where an action to which section 22B of this Act applies has not been brought within the period mentioned in subsection (2) of that section and the person subsequently dies in consequence of his injuries, an action to which this section applies shall not be competent in respect of those injuries or that death.

(5) Where a person would be entitled, but for this section, to bring an action for reparation other than one in which the damages claimed are confined to damages for loss of or damage to property, the court may, if it seems to it equitable to do so, allow him to bring the action notwithstanding this section.

(6) In this section 'relative' has the same meaning as in the Damages (Scotland) Act 1976.

(7) For the purposes of subsection (2)(b) above there shall be disregarded knowledge of whether particular facts and circumstances would or would not, as a matter of law, result in liability for damage under the said section 2.

Supplementary

Interpretation of this Part.

22D.—(1) Expressions used in this Part and in Part I of the 1987 Act shall have the same meanings in this Part as in the said Part I.

(2) For the purposes of section 1(1) of the 1987 Act, this Part shall have effect and be construed as if it were contained in Part I of that Act.

(3) In this Part, 'the 1987 Act' means the Consumer Protection Act 1987.''

11. Section 23 shall cease to have effect, but for the avoidance of doubt it is declared that the amendments in Part II of Schedule 4 shall continue to have effect.

12. In paragraph 2 of Schedule 1, after sub-paragraph (gg) there shall be inserted the following sub-paragraph—

"(ggg) to any obligation arising from liability under section 2 of the Consumer Protection Act 1987 (to make reparation for damage caused wholly or partly by a defect in a product);''.

SCHEDULE 2

PROHIBITION NOTICES AND NOTICES TO WARN

PART I

PROHIBITION NOTICES

1. A prohibition notice in respect of any goods shall—

    (a) state that the Secretary of State considers that the goods are unsafe;

    (b) set out the reasons why the Secretary of State considers that the goods are unsafe;

    (c) specify the day on which the notice is to come into force; and

    (d) state that the trader may at any time make representations in writing to the Secretary of State for the purpose of establishing that the goods are safe.

2.—(1) If representations in writing about a prohibition notice are made by the trader to the Secretary of State, it shall be the duty of the Secretary of State to consider whether to revoke the notice and—

    (a) if he decides to revoke it, to do so;

    (b) in any other case, to appoint a person to consider those representations, any further representations made (whether in writing or orally) by the trader about the notice and the statements of any witnesses examined under this Part of this Schedule.

(2) Where the Secretary of State has appointed a person to consider representations about a prohibition notice, he shall serve a notification on the trader which—

(a) states that the trader may make oral representations to the appointed person for the purpose of establishing that the goods to which the notice relates are safe; and

(b) specifies the place and time at which the oral representations may be made.

(3) The time specified in a notification served under sub-paragraph (2) above shall not be before the end of the period of twenty-one days beginning with the day on which the notification is served, unless the trader otherwise agrees.

(4) A person on whom a notification has been served under sub-paragraph (2) above or his representative may, at the place and time specified in the notification—

(a) make oral representations to the appointed person for the purpose of establishing that the goods in question are safe; and

(b) call and examine witnesses in connection with the representations.

3.—(1) Where representations in writing about a prohibition notice are made by the trader to the Secretary of State at any time after a person has been appointed to consider representations about that notice, then, whether or not the appointed person has made a report to the Secretary of State, the following provisions of this paragraph shall apply instead of paragraph 2 above.

(2) The Secretary of State shall, before the end of the period of one month beginning with the day on which he receives the representations, serve a notification on the trader which states—

(a) that the Secretary of State has decided to revoke the notice, has decided to vary it or, as the case may be, has decided neither to revoke nor to vary it; or

(b) that, a person having been appointed to consider representations about the notice, the trader may, at a place and time specified in the notification, make oral representations to the appointed person for the purpose of establishing that the goods to which the notice relates are safe.

(3) The time specified in a notification served for the purposes of sub-paragraph (2)(b) above shall not be before the end of the period of twenty-one days beginning with the day on which the notification is served, unless the trader otherwise agrees or the time is the time already specified for the purposes of paragraph 2(2)(b) above.

(4) A person on whom a notification has been served for the purposes of sub-paragraph (2)(b) above or his representative may, at the place and time specified in the notification—

(a) make oral representations to the appointed person for the purpose of establishing that the goods in question are safe; and

(b) call and examine witnesses in connection with the representations.

4.—(1) Where a person is appointed to consider representations about a prohibition notice, it shall be his duty to consider—

(a) any written representations made by the trader about the notice, other than those in respect of which a notification is served under paragraph 3(2)(a) above;

(b)   any oral representations made under paragraph 2(4) or 3(4) above; and

(c)   any statements made by witnesses in connection with the oral representations,

and, after considering any matters under this paragraph, to make a report (including recommendations) to the Secretary of State about the matters considered by him and the notice.

(2) It shall be the duty of the Secretary of State to consider any report made to him under sub-paragraph (1) above and, after considering the report, to inform the trader of his decision with respect to the prohibition notice to which the report relates.

5.—(1) The Secretary of State may revoke or vary a prohibition notice by serving on the trader a notification stating that the notice is revoked or, as the case may be, is varied as specified in the notification.

(2) The Secretary of State shall not vary a prohibition notice so as to make the effect of the notice more restrictive for the trader.

(3) Without prejudice to the power conferred by section 13(2) of this Act, the service of a notification under sub-paragraph (1) above shall be sufficient to satisfy the requirement of paragraph 4(2) above that the trader shall be informed of the Secretary of State's decision.

PART II

NOTICES TO WARN

6.—(1) If the Secretary of State proposes to serve a notice to warn on any person in respect of any goods, the Secretary of State, before he serves the notice, shall serve on that person a notification which—

(a)   contains a draft of the proposed notice;

(b)   states that the Secretary of State proposes to serve a notice in the form of the draft on that person;

(c)   states that the Secretary of State considers that the goods described in the draft are unsafe;

(d)   sets out the reasons why the Secretary of State considers that those goods are unsafe; and

(e)   states that that person may make representations to the Secretary of State for the purpose of establishing that the goods are safe if, before the end of the period of fourteen days beginning with the day on which the notification is served, he informs the Secretary of State—

(i)   of his intention to make representations; and

(ii)   whether the representations will be made only in writing or both in writing and orally.

(2) Where the Secretary of State has served a notification containing a draft of a proposed notice to warn on any person, he shall not serve a notice to warn on that person in respect of the goods to which the proposed notice relates unless—

(a)   the period of fourteen days beginning with the day on which the notification was served expires without the Secretary of State being informed as mentioned in sub-paragraph (1)(e) above;

(b)   the period of twenty-eight days beginning with that day expires without any written representations being made by that person to the Secretary of State about the proposed notice; or

(c)   the Secretary of State has considered a report about the proposed
        notice by a person appointed under paragraph 7(1) below.

7.—(1) Where a person on whom a notification containing a draft of a proposed notice to warn has been served—

(a)   informs the Secretary of State as mentioned in paragraph 6(1)(e) above before the end of the period of fourteen days beginning with the day on which the notification was served; and

(b)   makes written representations to the Secretary of State about the proposed notice before the end of the period of twenty-eight days beginning with that day,

the Secretary of State shall appoint a person to consider those representations, any further representations made by that person about the draft notice and the statements of any witnesses examined under this Part of this Schedule.

(2) Where—

(a)   the Secretary of State has appointed a person to consider representations about a proposed notice to warn; and

(b)   the person whose representations are to be considered has informed the Secretary of State for the purposes of paragraph 6(1)(e) above that the representations he intends to make will include oral representations,

the Secretary of State shall inform the person intending to make the representations of the place and time at which oral representations may be made to the appointed person.

(3) Where a person on whom a notification containing a draft of a proposed notice to warn has been served is informed of a time for the purposes of sub-paragraph (2) above, that time shall not be—

(a)   before the end of the period of twenty-eight days beginning with the day on which the notification was served; or

(b)   before the end of the period of seven days beginning with the day on which that person is informed of the time.

(4) A person who has been informed of a place and time for the purposes of sub-paragraph (2) above or his representative may, at that place and time—

(a)   make oral representations to the appointed person for the purpose of establishing that the goods to which the proposed notice relates are safe; and

(b)   call and examine witnesses in connection with the representations.

8.—(1) Where a person is appointed to consider representations about a proposed notice to warn, it shall be his duty to consider—

(a)   any written representations made by the person on whom it is proposed to serve the notice; and

(b)   in a case where a place and time has been appointed under paragraph 7(2) above for oral representations to be made by that person or his representative, any representations so made and any statements made by witnesses in connection with those representations,

and, after considering those matters, to make a report (including recommendations) to the Secretary of State about the matters considered by him and the proposal to serve the notice.

(2) It shall be the duty of the Secretary of State to consider any report made to him under sub-paragraph (1) above and, after considering the report, to inform the person on whom it was proposed that a notice to warn should be served of his decision with respect to the proposal.

(3) If at any time after serving a notification on a person under paragraph 6 above the Secretary of State decides not to serve on that person either the proposed notice to warn or that notice with modifications, the Secretary of State shall inform that person of the decision; and nothing done for the purposes of any of the preceding provisions of this Part of this Schedule before that person was so informed shall—

(a) entitle the Secretary of State subsequently to serve the proposed notice or that notice with modifications; or

(b) require the Secretary of State, or any person appointed to consider representations about the proposed notice, subsequently to do anything in respect of, or in consequence of, any such representations.

(4) Where a notification containing a draft of a proposed notice to warn is served on a person in respect of any goods, a notice to warn served on him in consequence of a decision made under sub-paragraph (2) above shall either be in the form of the draft or shall be less onerous than the draft.

9. The Secretary of State may revoke a notice to warn by serving on the person on whom the notice was served a notification stating that the notice is revoked.

PART III

GENERAL

10.—(1) Where in a notification served on any person under this Schedule the Secretary of State has appointed a time for the making of oral representations or the examination of witnesses, he may, by giving that person such notification as the Secretary of State considers appropriate, change that time to a later time or appoint further times at which further representations may be made or the examination of witnesses may be continued; and paragraphs 2(4), 3(4) and 7(4) above shall have effect accordingly.

(2) For the purposes of this Schedule the Secretary of State may appoint a person (instead of the appointed person) to consider any representations or statements, if the person originally appointed, or last appointed under this sub-paragraph, to consider those representations or statements has died or appears to the Secretary of State to be otherwise unable to act.

11. In this Schedule—

"the appointed person" in relation to a prohibition notice or a proposal to serve a notice to warn, means the person for the time being appointed under this Schedule to consider representations about the notice or, as the case may be, about the proposed notice;

"notification" means a notification in writing;

"trader", in relation to a prohibition notice, means the person on whom the notice is or was served.

SCHEDULE 3

AMENDMENTS OF PART I OF THE HEALTH AND SAFETY AT WORK ETC. ACT 1974

1.—(1) Section 6 (general duties of manufacturers etc. as regard articles and substances for use at work) shall be amended as follows.

(2) For subsection (1) (general duties of designers, manufacturers, importers and suppliers of articles for use at work) there shall be substituted the following subsections—

"(1) It shall be the duty of any person who designs, manufactures, imports or supplies any article for use at work or any article of fairground equipment—

    (a) to ensure, so far as is reasonably practicable, that the article is so designed and constructed that it will be safe and without risks to health at all times when it is being set, used, cleaned or maintained by a person at work;

    (b) to carry out or arrange for the carrying out of such testing and examination as may be necessary for the performance of the duty imposed on him by the preceding paragraph;

    (c) to take such steps as are necessary to secure that persons supplied by that person with the article are provided with adequate information about the use for which the article is designed or has been tested and about any conditions necessary to ensure that it will be safe and without risks to health at all such times as are mentioned in paragraph (a) above and when it is being dismantled or disposed of; and

    (d) to take such steps as are necessary to secure, so far as is reasonably practicable, that persons so supplied are provided with all such revisions of information provided to them by virtue of the preceding paragraph as are necessary by reason of its becoming known that anything gives rise to a serious risk to health or safety.

(1A) It shall be the duty of any person who designs, manufactures, imports or supplies any article of fairground equipment—

    (a) to ensure, so far as is reasonably practicable, that the article is so designed and constructed that it will be safe and without risks to health at all times when it is being used for or in connection with the entertainment of members of the public;

    (b) to carry out or arrange for the carrying out of such testing and examination as may be necessary for the performance of the duty imposed on him by the preceding paragraph;

    (c) to take such steps as are necessary to secure that persons supplied by that person with the article are provided with adequate information about the use for which the article is designed or has been tested and about any conditions necessary to ensure that it will be safe and without risks to health at all times when it is being used for or in connection with the entertainment of members of the public; and

    (d) to take such steps as are necessary to secure, so far as is reasonably practicable, that persons so supplied are provided with all such revisions of information provided to them by virtue of the preceding paragraph as are necessary by reason of its becoming known that anything gives rise to a serious risk to health or safety."

(3) In subsection (2) (duty of person who undertakes the design or manufacture of an article for use at work to carry out research), after the word "work" there shall be inserted the words "or of any article of fairground equipment".

(4) In subsection (3) (duty of persons who erect or install articles for use at work)—

(a) after the words "persons at work" there shall be inserted the words "or who erects or installs any article of fairground equipment"; and

(b) for the words from "it is" onwards there shall be substituted the words "the article is erected or installed makes it unsafe or a risk to health at any such time as is mentioned in paragraph (a) of subsection (1) or, as the case may be, in paragraph (a) of subsection (1) or (1A) above."

(5) For subsection (4) (general duties of manufacturers, importers and suppliers of substances for use at work) there shall be substituted the following subsection—

"(4) It shall be the duty of any person who manufactures, imports or supplies any substance—

(a) to ensure, so far as is reasonably practicable, that the substance will be safe and without risks to health at all times when it is being used, handled, processed, stored or transported by a person at work or in premises to which section 4 above applies;

(b) to carry out or arrange for the carrying out of such testing and examination as may be necessary for the performance of the duty imposed on him by the preceding paragraph;

(c) to take such steps as are necessary to secure that persons supplied by that person with the substance are provided with adequate information about any risks to health or safety to which the inherent properties of the substance may give rise, about the results of any relevant tests which have been carried out on or in connection with the substance and about any conditions necessary to ensure that the substance will be safe and without risks to health at all such times as are mentioned in paragraph (a) above and when the substance is being disposed of; and

(d) to take such steps as are necessary to secure, so far as is reasonably practicable, that persons so supplied are provided with all such revisions of information provided to them by virtue of the preceding paragraph as are necessary by reason of its becoming known that anything gives rise to a serious risk to health or safety."

(6) In subsection (5) (duty of person who undertakes the manufacture of a substance for use at work to carry out research)—

(a) for the words "substance for use at work" there shall be substituted the word "substance"; and

(b) at the end there shall be inserted the words "at all such times as are mentioned in paragraph (a) of subsection (4) above".

(7) In subsection (8) (relief from duties for persons relying on undertakings by others)—

(a) for the words "for or to another" there shall be substituted the words "for use at work or an article of fairground equipment and does so for or to another";

(b) for the words "when properly used" there shall be substituted the words "at all such times as are mentioned in paragraph (a) of subsection (1) or, as the case may be, in paragraph (a) of subsection (1) or (1A) above"; and

(c) for the words "by subsection (1)(a) above" there shall be substituted the words "by virtue of that paragraph".

(8) After the said subsection (8) there shall be inserted the following subsection—

"(8A) Nothing in subsection (7) or (8) above shall relieve any person who imports any article or substance from any duty in respect of anything which—

(a) in the case of an article designed outside the United Kingdom, was done by and in the course of any trade, profession or other undertaking carried on by, or was within the control of, the person who designed the article; or

(b) in the case of an article or substance manufactured outside the United Kingdom, was done by and in the course of any trade, profession or other undertaking carried on by, or was within the control of, the person who manufactured the article or substance."

(9) In subsection (9) (definition of supplier in certain cases of supply under a hire-purchase agreement), for the words "article for use at work or substance for use at work" there shall be substituted the words "article or substance".

(10) For subsection (10) (meaning of "properly used") there shall be substituted the following subsection—

"(10) For the purposes of this section an absence of safety or a risk to health shall be disregarded in so far as the case in or in relation to which it would arise is shown to be one the occurrence of which could not reasonably be foreseen; and in determining whether any duty imposed by virtue of paragraph (a) of subsection (1), (1A) or (4) above has been performed regard shall be had to any relevant information or advice which has been provided to any person by the person by whom the article has been designed, manufactured, imported or supplied or, as the case may be, by the person by whom the substance has been manufactured, imported or supplied."

2. In section 22 (prohibition notices)—

(a) in subsections (1) and (2) (notices in respect of activities which are or are about to be carried on and involve a risk of serious personal injury), for the word "about", in each place where it occurs, there shall be substituted the word "likely";

(b) for subsection (4) (notice to have immediate effect only if the risk is imminent) there shall be substituted the following subsection—

"(4) A direction contained in a prohibition notice in pursuance of subsection (3)(d) above shall take effect—

(a) at the end of the period specified in the notice; or

(b) if the notice so declares, immediately."

3. After section 25 there shall be inserted the following section—

"Power of customs officer to detain articles and substances.

25A.—(1) A customs officer may, for the purpose of facilitating the exercise or performance by any enforcing authority or inspector of any of the powers or duties of the authority or inspector under any of the relevant statutory provisions, seize any imported article or imported substance and detain it for not more than two working days.

(2) Anything seized and detained under this section shall be dealt with during the period of its detention in such manner as the Commissioners of Customs and Excise may direct.

(3) In subsection (1) above the reference to two working days is a reference to a period of forty-eight hours calculated from the time when the goods in question are seized but disregarding so much of any period as falls on a Saturday or Sunday or on Chistmas Day, Good Friday or a day which is a bank holiday under the Banking and Financial Dealings Act 1971 in the part of Great Britain where the goods are seized."

4. After section 27 (power to obtain information) there shall be inserted the following section—

"Information communicated by the Commissioners of Customs and Excise.

27A.—(1) If they think it appropriate to do so for the purpose of facilitating the exercise or performance by any person to whom subsection (2) below applies of any of that person's powers or duties under any of the relevant statutory provisions, the Commissioners of Customs and Excise may authorise the disclosure to that person of any information obtained for the purposes of the exercise by the Commissioners of their functions in relation to imports.

(2) This subsection applies to an enforcing authority and to an inspector.

(3) A disclosure of information made to any person under subsection (1) above shall be made in such manner as may be directed by the Commissioners of Customs and Excise and may be made through such persons acting on behalf of that person as may be so directed.

(4) Information may be disclosed to a person under subsection (1) above whether or not the disclosure of the information has been requested by or on behalf of that person."

5. In section 28 (restrictions on disclosure of information), in subsection (1)(a), after the words "furnished to any person" there shall be inserted the words "under section 27A above or".

6. In section 33(1)(h) (offence of obstructing an inspector), after the word "duties" there shall be inserted the words "or to obstruct a customs officer in the exercise of his powers under section 25A".

7. In section 53(1) (general interpretation of Part I)—

(a) after the definition of "article for use at work" there shall be inserted the following definition—

" 'article of fairground equipment' means any fairground equipment or any article designed for use as a component in any such equipment;"

(b) after the definition of "credit-sale agreement" there shall be inserted the following definition—

" 'customs officer' means an officer within the meaning of the Customs and Excise Management Act 1979;"

(c) before the definition of "the general purposes of this Part" there shall be inserted the following definition—

" 'fairground equipment' means any fairground ride, any similar plant which is designed to be in motion for entertainment purposes with members of the public on or inside it or any plant which is designed to be used by members of the public for entertainment purposes either as a slide or for bouncing upon, and in this definition the reference to plant which is designed to be in motion with members of the public on or inside it includes a reference to swings, dodgems and other plant which is designed to be in motion wholly or partly under the control of, or to be put in motion by, a member of the public;"

(d) after the definition of "local authority" there shall be inserted the following definition—

"'micro-organism' includes any microscopic biological entity which is capable of replication;"

(e) in the definition of "substance", after the words "natural or artificial substance" there shall be inserted the words "(including micro-organisms)".

SCHEDULE 4

Section 48.

MINOR AND CONSEQUENTIAL AMENDMENTS

The Explosives Act 1875

1875 c. 17.

1. In sections 31 and 80 of the Explosives Act 1875 (prohibitions on selling gunpowder to children and on use of fireworks in public places), for the words from "shall be liable" onwards there shall be substituted the words "shall be guilty of an offence and liable on summary conviction to a fine not exceeding level 5 on the standard scale".

The Trade Descriptions Act 1968

1968 c. 29.

2.—(1) In section 2 of the Trade Descriptions Act 1968 (meaning of trade description)—

(a) for paragraph (g) of subsection (4) (marks and descriptions applied in pursuance of the Consumer Safety Act 1978) there shall be substituted   1978 c. 38. the following paragraph—

"(g) the Consumer Protection Act 1987;" and

(b) in subsection (5)(a) (descriptions prohibited under certain enactments), for the words "or the Consumer Safety Act 1978" there shall be substituted the words "or the Consumer Protection Act 1987".

(2) In section 28(5A) of the said Act of 1968 (disclosure of information authorised for purpose specified in section 174(3) of the Consumer Credit Act   1974 c.39. 1974), for the words from "section 174(3)" onwards there shall be substituted the words "section 38(2)(a), (b) or (c) of the Consumer Protection Act 1987."

The Fair Trading Act 1973

1973 c. 41.

3. In section 130(1) of the Fair Trading Act 1973 (notice of intended prosecution by weights and measures authority to Director General of Fair Trading), after the words "that Act," there shall be inserted the words "or for an offence under any provision made by or under Part III of the Consumer Protection Act 1987,".

The Consumer Credit Act 1974

1974 c. 39.

4. In section 174(3)(a) of the Consumer Credit Act 1974 (exceptions to general restrictions on disclosure of information), after the words "or the Airports Act   1986 c.31. 1986" there shall be inserted the words "or the Consumer Protection Act 1987".

The Torts (Interference with Goods) Act 1977

1977 c. 32.   5. In section 1 of the Torts (Interference with Goods) Act 1977 (meaning of "wrongful interference"), after paragraph (d) there shall be inserted the following words—

> "and references in this Act (however worded) to proceedings for wrongful interference or to a claim or right to claim for wrongful interference shall include references to proceedings by virtue of Part I of the Consumer Protection Act 1987 (product liability) in respect of any damage to goods or to an interest in goods or, as the case may be, to a claim or right to claim by virtue of that Part in respect of any such damage."

1979 c. 38.   *The Estate Agents Act 1979*

6. In section 10(3)(a) of the Estate Agents Act 1979 (exceptions to general restrictions on disclosure of information), after the words "or the Airports Act 1986" there shall be inserted the words "or the Consumer Protection Act 1987."

1980 c. 21.   *The Competition Act 1980*

7. In section 19(3) of the Competition Act 1980 (enactments specified in exceptions to general restrictions on disclosure of information), after paragraph (i) there shall be inserted the following paragraph—

> "(j) the Consumer Protection Act 1987."

1982 c. 46.   *The Employment Act 1982*

8. In section 16(2) of the Employment Act 1982 (proceedings against trade unions in relation to which the appropriate limit does not apply), after paragraph (b) there shall be inserted the following words—

> "or to any proceedings by virtue of Part I of the Consumer Protection Act 1987 (product liability)."

1984 c. 12.   *The Telecommunications Act 1984*

9.—(1) In sections 28(6) and 85(5)(b) of the Telecommunications Act 1984 (meaning of "supply"), for the words "be construed in accordance with section 9 of the Consumer Safety Act 1978" there shall be substituted the words "have the same meaning as it has in Part II of the Consumer Protection Act 1987".

(2) In section 101(3) of the said Act of 1984 (enactments specified in exceptions to general restrictions on disclosure of information), after paragraph (g) there shall be inserted the following paragraph—

> "(h) the Consumer Protection Act 1987."

1986 c. 31.   *The Airports Act 1986*

10. In section 74(3) of the Airports Act 1986 (enactments specified in exceptions to general restrictions on disclosure of information), after paragraph (h) there shall be inserted the following paragraph—

> "(i) the Consumer Protection Act 1987."

1986 c. 44.   *The Gas Act 1986*

11. In section 42 of the Gas Act 1986—

(a) in subsection (3) (restrictions on disclosure of information except for the purposes of certain enactments), at the end there shall be inserted the following paragraph—

"(j) the Consumer Protection Act 1987.";

(b) after subsection (5) there shall be inserted the following subsection—

"(6) In relation to the Consumer Protection Act 1987 the reference in subsection (2)(b) above to a weights and measures authority shall include a reference to any person on whom functions under that Act are conferred by regulations under section 27(2) of that Act."

The Insolvency Act 1986

12. In section 281(5)(a) of the Insolvency Act 1986 (discharge from bankruptcy not to release bankrupt from liability in respect of personal injuries), for the word "being" there shall be substituted the words "or to pay damages by virtue of Part I of the Consumer Protection Act 1987, being in either case".

The Motor Cycle Noise Act 1987

13. For paragraphs 3 to 5 of the Schedule to the Motor Cycle Noise Act 1987 (enforcement) there shall be substituted the following paragraph—

"3. Part IV of the Consumer Protection Act 1987 (enforcement), except section 31 (power of customs officers to detain goods), shall have effect as if the provisions of this Act were safety provisions within the meaning of that Act; and in Part V of that Act (miscellaneous and supplemental), except in section 49 (Northern Ireland), references to provisions of the said Part IV shall include references to those provisions as applied by this paragraph."

SCHEDULE 5

REPEALS

Chapter	Short title	Extent of repeal
3 & 4 Geo. 5. c. 17.	The Fabrics (Misdescription) Act 1913.	The whole Act.
1967 c. 80.	The Criminal Justice Act 1967.	In Part I of Schedule 3, the entry relating to the Fabrics (Misdescription) Act 1913.
1967 c. 29. (N.I.).	The Fines Act (Northern Ireland) 1967.	In Part I of the Schedule, the entry relating to the Fabrics (Misdescription) Act 1913.
1968 c. 29.	The Trade Descriptions Act 1968.	Section 11.
1972 c. 34.	The Trade Descriptions Act 1972.	The whole Act.
1972 c. 70.	The Local Government Act 1972.	In Part II of Schedule 29, paragraph 18(1).
1973 c. 52.	The Prescription and Limitation (Scotland) Act 1973.	Section 23.
1973 c. 65.	The Local Government (Scotland) Act 1973.	In Part II of Schedule 27, paragraph 50.
1974 c. 37.	The Health and Safety at Work etc. Act 1974.	In section 53(1), the definition of "substance for use at work".
1976 c. 26.	The Explosives (Age of Purchase etc.) Act 1976.	In section 1, in subsection (1), the words from "and for the word" onwards and subsection (2).
1978 c. 38.	The Consumer Safety Act 1978.	The whole Act.
1980 c. 43.	The Magistrates' Courts Act 1980.	In Schedule 7, paragraphs 172 and 173.
1984 c. 12.	The Telecommunications Act 1984.	In section 101(3)(f), the word "and".
1984 c. 30.	The Food Act 1984.	In Schedule 10, paragraph 32.
1986 c. 29.	The Consumer Safety (Amendment) Act 1986.	The whole Act.
1986 c. 31.	The Airports Act 1986.	In section 74(3)(g), the word "and".
1986 c. 44.	The Gas Act 1986.	In section 42(3), paragraphs (a) and (g) and, in paragraph (h), the word "and".

Appendix 3

The Brussels Convention 1968 on jurisdiction and the enforcement of judgments, Articles 1 to 6A

Schedule 1 to the Civil Jurisdiction and Judgments Act 1982

TITLE I: SCOPE
Article 1
This Convention shall apply in civil and commercial matters whatever the nature of the court or tribunal. It shall not extend, in particular, to revenue, customs or administrative matters.

The Convention shall not apply to:
   (1) the status or legal capacity of natural persons, rights in property arising out of a matrimonial relationship, wills and succession;
   (2) bankruptcy, proceedings relating to the winding-up of insolvent companies or other legal persons, judicial arrangements, compositions and analogous proceedings;
   (3) social security;
   (4) arbitration.

TITLE II: JURISDICTION
Section 1: General provisions

Article 2
Subject to the provisions of this Convention, persons domiciled in a Contracting State shall, whatever their nationality, be sued in the courts of that State.

Persons who are not nationals of the State in which they are domiciled shall be governed by the rules of jurisdiction applicable to nationals of that State.

Article 3

Persons domiciled in a Contracting State may be sued in the courts of another Contracting State only by virtue of the rules set out in Sections 2 to 6 of this Title.

In particular the following provisions shall not be applicable as against them:

-in Belgium:	Article 15 of the civil code (*Code civil-Burgerlijk Wetboek*) and Article 638 of the Judicial code (*Code judiciaire- Gerechtelijk Wetboek*);
-in Denmark:	Article 248(2) of the law on civil procedure (*Lov om rettens pleje*) and Chapter 3, Article 3 of the Greenland law on civil procedure (*Lov for Gronland om rettens pleje);*
-in the Federal Republic of Germany:	Article 23 of the code of civil procedure (*Zivilprozessordnung);*
-in France:	Articles 14 and 15 of the civil code (*Code civil*);
-in Ireland:	the rules which enable jurisdiction to be founded on the document instituting the proceedings having been served on the defendant during his temporary presence in Ireland;
-in Italy:	Article 2 and Article 4, Nos 1 and 2 of the code of civil procedure (*Codice di procedura civile);*
-in Luxembourg:	Articles 14 and 15 of the civil code (*Code civil*);
-in the Netherlands:	Article 126(3) and Article 127 of the code of civil procedure (*Wetboek van Burgerlijke Rechtsvordering);*
-in the United Kingdom	the rules which enable jurisdiction to be founded on: (a) the document instituting the proceedings having been served on the defendant during his temporary presence in the United Kingdom; or

(b) the presence within the United Kingdom of property belonging to the defendant; or
(c) the seizure by the plaintiff of property situated in the United Kingdom.

Article 4

If the defendant is not domiciled in a Contracting State, the jurisdiction of the courts of each Contracting State shall, subject to the provisions of Article 16, be determined by the law of that State.

As against such a defendant, any person domiciled in a Contracting State may, whatever his nationality, avail himself in that State of the rules of jurisdiction there in force, and in particular those specified in the second paragraph of Article 3, in the same way as the nationals of that State.

Section 2: Special jurisdiction

Article 5

A person domiciled in a Contracting State may, in another Contracting State, be sued:

(1) in matters relating to a contract, in the courts for the place of performance of the obligation in question;

(2) in matters relating to maintenance, in the courts for the place where the maintenance creditor is domiciled or habitually resident or, if the matter is ancillary to proceedings concerning the status of a person, in the court which, according to its own law, has jurisdiction to entertain those proceedings, unless that jurisdiction is based solely on the nationality of one of the parties;

(3) in matters relating to tort, delict or quasi-delict, in the courts for the place where the harmful event occurred;

(4) as regards a civil claim for damages or restitution which is based on an act giving rise to criminal proceedings, in the court seised of those proceedings, to the extent that that court has jurisdiction under its own law to entertain civil proceedings;

(5) as regards a dispute arising out of the operations of a branch, agency or other establishment, in the courts for the place in which the branch, agency or other establishment is situated;

(6) in his capacity as settlor, trustee or beneficiary of a trust created by the operation of a statute, or by a written instrument, or created orally and evidenced in writing, in the courts of the

Contracting State in which the trust is domiciled;
(7) as regards a dispute concerning the payment of remuneration claimed in respect of the salvage of a cargo or freight, in the court under the authority of which the cargo or freight in question:
   (a) has been arrested to secure such payment, or
   (b) could have been so arrested, but bail or other security has been given;

provided that this provision shall apply only if it is claimed that the defendant has an interest in the cargo or freight or had such an interest at the time of salvage.

Article 6
A person domiciled in a Contracting State may also be sued:
(1) where he is one of a number of defendants, in the courts for the place where any one of them is domiciled;
(2) as a third party in an action on a warranty or guarantee or in any other third party proceedings, in the court seised of the original proceedings, unless these were instituted solely with the object of removing him from the jurisdiction of the court which would be competent in his case;
(3) on a counterclaim arising from the same contract or facts on which the original claim was based, in the court in which the original claim is pending.

Article 6A
Where by virtue of this Convention a court of a Contracting State has jurisdiction in actions relating to liability arising from the use or operation of a ship, that court, or any other court substituted for this purpose by the internal law of that State, shall also have jurisdiction over claims for limitation of such liability.

Bibliography

Benjamin: Sale of Goods, 3rd edition 1987
Chalmers' Sale of Goods Act 1979, 18th edition 1981
Clerk & Lindsell: Torts, 15th edition 1982
Department of Trade & Industry: Implementation of EC Directive on
    Product Liability: An explanatory and consultative note, 1985
EC Commission: Report on Product Liability (s11/76)
Hartley: Civil Jurisdiction and Judgments, 1984
Jenard: Report on the 1968 Convention
Miller: Product Liability and Safety Encyclopedia, 1987
Salmond & Heuston: Law of Tort, 18th edition 1981
Whincup: Product Liability Law, 1985

Index

INDEX